One-Minute Monologues for Teens

100 Original Monologues

One-Minute Monologues for Teens

100 Original Monologues

Mike Kimmel
Foreword by Paris Smith

ISBN 13: 978-0-9981513-8-0

Ben Rose Creative Arts
New York - Los Angeles

Printed in the United States of America
First Edition

Publisher's Cataloging-in-Publication Data
provided by Five Rainbows Cataloging Services

Names: Kimmel, Mike, author. | Smith, Paris, writer of foreword.
Title: One-minute monologues for teens : 100 original monologues / Mike Kimmel ; foreword by Paris Smith.
Description: Los Angeles : Ben Rose Creative Arts, 2020. | Audience: Grades 9-12.
Identifiers: ISBN 978-0-9981513-8-0 (paperback) | ISBN 978-0-9981513-9-7 (ebook : epub) | ISBN 978-1-953057-99-0 (ebook : mobi)
Subjects: LCSH: Monologues–Juvenile literature. | Acting–Auditions–Juvenile literature. | Comedy–Juvenile literature. | Drama–Juvenile literature. | Arts–Study and teaching. | BISAC: YOUNG ADULT NONFICTION / Performing Arts / General. | PERFORMING ARTS / Monologues & Scenes. | PERFORMING ARTS / Acting & Auditioning. | EDUCATION / Arts in Education.
Classification: LCC PN2080 .K56 2020 (print) | LCC PN2080 (ebook) | DDC 812/.6–dc23.

Praise for
One-Minute Monologues for Teens

"As talent agents, we are always being asked about practice materials for honing skills of all our performers, but with Mike Kimmel's ***One-Minute Monologues for Teens***, he provides relevant material that connects with our youth in real life situations and outcomes that promote morals, ethics and values that our teens can actually apply in real life situations. SWAG proudly endorses ***One-Minute Monologues for Teens*** and will always have a copy in our resource library. We think every youth instructor/school should too!"

~ Mina Lara and Katrina Fristoe
South West Artist Group
A SAG/AFTRA Franchised Talent Agency
Arizona, Utah, and New Mexico

"I don't know how Mike Kimmel does it, but he captures the voice and thoughts of teenagers perfectly! Is there a 14 year old ghost writer hiding in his office? These monologues are uber-modern, age-relatable, and I was pleasantly surprised at how inspirational they are. As someone who started acting in grade school, I wish I had a book like this, instead of all that typical outdated adult material that was given."

~ Tanjareen Thomas
Actor and Producer
Portrays Brandy on Freeform's *Famous in Love*
Portrays Rachel on Bounce TV's *Family Time*
Insecure, Curb Your Enthusiasm, Funny Married Stuff, Miss March, Days of Our Lives, According to Jim, Strong Medicine, NYPD Blue, Becker, Arli$$, V.I.P., The Jenny McCarthy Show, Girlfriends

"Mike Kimmel and I have known and acted with each other for twenty years in Los Angeles. I have taught at the Young Actors Theatre Camp for 15 years and have guest taught at USC's School of Cinema. Mike and I are both passionate about young performers' success in the Arts and his books help in that quest."

~ Tracy Weisert
Actor and Acting Coach
Superstore, Joe Dirt 2, Tosh.O, Monk, The Neighbors, Gone Girl, ER, Wyatt Earp, Wild Wild West, Cabot College, Life in Pieces, Adam Ruins Everything, Off the Menu

"*One-Minute Monologues for Teens* is a solid collection of scripts that will be very helpful for young actors, as well as their teachers and coaches. In my years of training as an actor and martial artist, I've learned to recognize and appreciate the value of discipline, study, and focus. This book will be an effective tool to assist young actors with their own training and development."

~ Cynthia Rothrock
Actor and World-Renowned Martial Artist
Guardian Angel, Eye for an Eye, Honor and Glory,
No Way Back, Martial Law, China O'Brien, Sci-Fighter,
Night Vision, Showdown in Manila, Tiger Claws,
Hercules: The Legendary Journeys

"Mike Kimmel's new book **One-Minute Monologues For Teens** is unique because it offers teenage actors and actresses the chance to audition with short monologues that deal with topics such as cell phones, teacher crushes, school, and learning about the craft of acting. Much like short films, Kimmel's short monologues are a wonderful tool for young performers to showcase their skill set with brevity, short, sweet and to the point."

~ Katharine "Kat" Kramer
Actress/Singer/Writer/Producer/ Influencer
Kat Kramer's Films That Change The World
KNK Productions, Inc./ Stanley Kramer Library
Turnover, Little Fockers, Mother's Day Memories,
Civil Disobedience, Child of the '70s

"Mike Kimmel does it again. This book explodes with positivity. Teens need this material! It is good to know that we are sending them out into show biz with a strong, healthy identity using those powerful containers called 'words.' Thank you, Mike, for another powerful monologue book!"

~ GiGi Erneta
Actor, Host, and Producer
Happy Death Day, Happy Death Day 2U, Roswell, New Mexico, Flag of My Father, When the Bough Breaks, Risen, Nashville, The First, Jane the Virgin, VEEP, Scandal, American Crime, Queen of the South, Body Cam, NCIS New Orleans, Dallas, The Purge, Strong Medicine, Friday Night Lights, Veronica Mars

"Folks, this Mike Kimmel knows how to write. He's done it again and this time for teens. As I was reading the advance material, I realized they are not just well thought-out monologues for teens in an acting class. This book is filled with positive messages and words of wisdom, plus you also get the Mighty Mike humor. Congrats to my friend I first met when we were doing a skit with Jay Leno on *The Tonight Show*. Congrats to teens too – you've got another entertaining book to help you with training and auditions."

~ Ben McCain
Actor, TV Host, and Producer
My Name is Bruce, House of Cards, Homecoming, Bio-Dome, Martial Law, Black Scorpion, Nashville Now, Lois and Clark: The New Adventures of Superman, Julian, The Pretender, Dead End, Hee Haw, Killer Tumbleweeds

"Mike Kimmel has a way of writing enjoyable, uplifting and good-natured monologues. Not only are they written from a cool perspective, but they are thought-provoking for both the teen actor and the audience member. In fact, it is truly remarkable how he manages to incorporate such intuitive and inspirational content in one-minute monologues that are relatable to teen actors, as well as very relevant to our current time. It's always refreshing to find monologues that are new, interesting, and something you can ultimately make your own. Teens will love these!!"

~ Gwendolynn Murphy
Dallas Mavericks Dancers Alumni
Theater, Film, TV and Voice Over Actress
Murder Made Me Famous, No Ordinary Love, Breakers
The Witches of the Watch, The Harrowing, The Crimson Files
The Deep End, Walker, Texas Ranger, Baba Yaga, Glow

"There's an innocence and simplicity in Mike Kimmel's monologues that you don't often find when seeking good acting material. You learn from his words. The discipline and tenacity in these texts present a positive outlook on life we so often crave. If you're going to memorize a piece, memorize something that speaks to you."

~ Cait Brasel
Actor and Director
Distant Vision, Francis Ford Coppola's Live Cinema Workshop,
Heaven's Rain, Mono, Mono Deux, Wolf Head, Silhouettes,
Electric Nostalgia, You People, Raghav, T-Rex, Binary Flower

For Gabriella, Julianna, and Dylan,
who always make me smile

"Everyone is unique and special in some way, and to think less of yourself is to slap the face of your Creator. You've been given gifts and it's time to make them real."

~ Anthony Robbins

Table of Contents

Mike Kimmel

Foreword

The moment when my dear friend, actor, and writer Mike Kimmel invited me to pen this brief foreword to his new book, *One-Minute Monologues for Teens*, I leapt at the opportunity. I am honored to have known Mike since I was seven years old, as he is truly one of the most genuine and gracious people I have had the privilege to know. In addition to being passionate about his craft, Mike is a brilliant actor, an insightful writer, and an inspiring, caring mentor to young teens who aspire to perform.

Actors are dreamers. It's in our blood. My personal journey has been somewhat nontraditional: I come from a conservative family of non-actors, but I was a very outgoing child with boundless energy. I performed whenever and for whomever I could: doing accents for strangers on airplanes, singing at the neighborhood lemonade stand, and even rapping for random shoppers in the mall.

As a child actor moving from provincial Texas to the bright lights of Hollywood, I had no idea what I was walking into. All I knew was that I wanted to act. I vividly remember thinking as I arrived in Hollywood–one hand on my hip and wearing a bow as large as my head–"This is my town and no one's running me out of here." I came to Los Angeles as a naive, sassy, and supremely confident eleven-year-old ready to take on the world.

The Hollywood in my head was so different from the one I encountered in real life. Reflecting on this experience now as an adult makes me feel grateful for the relationships I've made along the way. Working alongside talented directors, producers, writers, assistant directors, casting directors, cast members, wardrobe designers, hair and makeup artists, and crew members, I've seen firsthand how everyone becomes a family on set. In making these special connections, everybody works as a team to support one another. The magic of acting for me is in this collective effort to make art with a plethora of committed, inspiring artists. Acting is a challenging profession, but seeking out members of the community who have walked this path has uplifted me and made me feel part of a greater whole united by a dedication to the craft. Every actor has his or her own story – and this business does not provide a one-size-fits-all path to success. Yet there is something innate and deeply embedded in every actor that enables us to connect not only to each other as artists striving for something bigger than ourselves, but to the characters that we create and embody.

It is gratifying to know that people like Mike are writing books for young actors that incorporate tangible, and above all, actable and positive content. I understand the difficulties of finding high quality, conversational material for young people to utilize for auditions and showcases. I remember my constant search for monologues when I was younger. People respond differently to different pieces, and I love Mike's monologues because they are authentic for today's youth.

My approach to preparing for a new script varies with each character I play – but there are common elements that I employ consistently throughout my process. When breaking down a script and tackling each new scene, I try to relate deeply to my characters, while still distinguishing them from my true self. I ask myself these questions: "How am I different from my character? How am I the same? What do I want from the other people in the scene? What do I want to make them feel, and how do I want the audience to feel? How can I actively collaborate for the best possible experience for all?"

Another strategy I use is to translate the lines of dialogue into my own words to solidify the motivations of the characters and clarify the overarching structure of each scene. This exercise helps me better connect to the character from a place of truth. I also analyze the order in which the lines are laid out in a scene – asking: "Why does this line come next?" Stakes are critical in my work, as well. I always want to utilize high stakes because they keep me emotionally hooked into my action and connected to my objective. These high stakes, paired with clear objectives, allow me to always stay present and in the moment.

Finally, I love adding the element of improvisation to my work, because it frees me from whatever underlying fears and limitations I may have, such as the stakes, timing, or objectives of the scene. I will have a fellow actor improvise lines with me, making it up as we go – but staying in sequence with the circumstances and arc of the scene. This allows for a sense of playfulness and spontaneity in my work, which are essential components of acting.

Mike's monologues give the actor so much to play with and so much room for exploration and creativity. This is part of their magic. They are real and raw, and target human issues that are universal: any actor or audience member can relate to these pieces on some level. This lies in stark contrast to some of the practiced monologues of my youth, which lent themselves to over-acting. Mike's monologues carry inspiring and uplifting messages that will undoubtedly impact the fortunate ears that get to hear them. I am so happy to see monologues that shed a positive light on what really matters: compassion and humanity. Mike's monologues target topics that are relevant to the challenges teens face today and encourage them to think about doing the right thing. Some of them talk about not spending twenty-four hours a day on your phone, spending more time with family, and valuing self-worth and self-esteem.

I've come to know Mike well, and I think this book will speak to artists like myself who strive to be the best they can be in an industry defined by one word: rejection. The stream of "no's" can still be hard, but I never let rejection control my life. Mike uplifts the reader by emphasizing acceptance, love, and empathy in all of his writing. I see Mike as a true artist whose words connect the hearts and souls of impassioned artists. I'm so blessed to have learned so much from Mike, and I know that you will experience that same clarity through reading and performing his words.

Paris Smith
Los Angeles, California

Acknowledgments

As ever, a million thanks to my three wonderful sisters, Mollie, Adele, and Tammy. Their kindness, graciousness, and generosity are beyond description and beyond compare.

Many thanks to Kimberly Bliquez, GiGi Erneta, Tina and A.J. Guillot, Kat Kramer, Karen and Chrissy Pavlick, Cynthia Rothrock, Tanjareen Thomas, Erik Beelman, Stephen Bowling, David Breland, Francis Ford Coppola, Gene LeBell, Ben McCain, Morgan Roberts, Ben Rose, and William Wellman Jr. for their encouragement, support, and loyal friendship.

Very special thanks to my dear friend and colleague – and extraordinary actor – Paris Smith, for sharing her unique insights in the foreword to this book. Paris is a dedicated, diligent, and dynamic performing artist. She is an outstanding role model for young actors everywhere.

Introduction

The process of selecting, rehearsing, and performing monologues is one of the most challenging – and often misunderstood – areas of study in the entire world of acting and performance. Through the years, this has been especially true for newcomers to the entertainment industry. Monologues, however, are often requested as a necessary first step in the audition process for young actors. Talent agents, casting directors, and other entertainment industry professionals have come to rely heavily upon monologue performances to assist them in narrowing their choices among all the available actors in our highly competitive field.

However, performing monologues can be one of the most powerful ways for performers of all ages to represent themselves well – and put their best foot forward when stepping inside those audition rooms. Industry professionals look closely at an actor's choice of monologue to reveal subtle clues about that actor's unique character and personality. We're all wildly different. It should come as no surprise, then, that different actors are drawn towards very different types of performance material.

Actors have an opportunity to reinvent themselves continually through the creative study and application of new monologues. This is one of the most effective strategies, in fact, for showing industry folks – who may already know our work – entirely new and different aspects of our personalities. A talented comedian, for example, can show his serious side by performing a new dramatic monologue. Similarly, an actress normally drawn to more serious, dramatic material can introduce agents and casting directors to her lighter, more comedic side – and broaden her appeal – by making these industry professionals laugh.

Though many actors tend to favor either dramatic or comedic material exclusively, there is no reason why performers may not excel in both these areas. Ideally, actors should strive to become equally adept at both comedy and drama. There is certainly no practical reason for actors to consciously limit themselves to only one specialty area or the other. However, even very experienced actors – those with major industry credits and experience – often make this unfortunate mistake.

In this respect, actors should think of monologues as tools we can use to show industry professionals our very best sides – and thereby surprise them with our overall flexibility and versatility. At any given time, you have an opportunity to search through your toolbox – this book and your other monologue books – for a new performance piece that allows you to show yourself off in a new and different light to audiences, peers, teachers, and industry professionals alike.

Regardless of your personal preferences – comedy or drama – it is extremely important to perform every monologue in as conversational and naturalistic a style as possible. Try your best to "make the material your own." This is a very common expression in show business, but can often be confusing to newcomers. It is meant to help actors imagine that the words coming out of their mouths are their very own inventions – and originated as thoughts, ideas, feelings, and emotions in their very own minds.

Try to avoid the appearance, then, of being overly "presentational" when performing your monologue. There is a tendency among actors – particularly young actors – to approach a monologue like an important speech they are delivering to an invited audience. Some young people even treat acting monologues as though they were pieces intended for speech and debate class. This is understandable, but is also a fundamental mistake. This approach can often lead to performances that appear stiff, stilted, and somewhat unnatural in their delivery.

Young actors will be far more successful when they start thinking of their monologues as secrets they're sharing with close friends and relatives. Try your best, therefore, to imagine you're telling a secret or revealing something deeply personal about yourself with the words you're sharing in a monologue. This will go a long way towards helping you establish a strong sense of familiarity and personal connection with your audience.

Let me share a little-known secret about show business with you. Audiences truly want to see us succeed. The audience is on our side. Many people in life are afraid to speak and perform in public. Many people are also very shy and embarrassed about expressing their true feelings and emotions to others – both publicly and privately. This is especially true nowadays with our ever-increasing reliance upon technology. In recent years, there's been a dramatic decline in the overall quality of our basic conversational and interpersonal skills. Today, people are not nearly as comfortable (or effective) in expressing themselves verbally as they were in years past. Audiences are well aware of this uncomfortable and unfortunate decline. As a result, they tend to feel tremendous empathy with us as performers. Audiences, therefore, are strongly inclined to root for the actor on stage to succeed.

This is one of the most difficult concepts for actors to understand and accept, but I promise you that it's true. The audience – with very few exceptions – is absolutely, one hundred percent in your corner. Don't ever make the mistake of thinking that the audience is there to judge you. Instead, think of the audience as your own personal cheering section every time you step out to perform on stage – or in front of a camera. The audience wants very much to see you knock it out of the park. The audience wants to be "wowed." The audience is looking – and hoping – for a reason to leap to its collective feet and give you a standing ovation.

The one hundred monologues in this book have been specifically prepared with teenagers in mind. Many can be performed by younger actors and older actors, as well, but these pieces were written – and are primarily intended – for teens. They address topics relevant to today's teenager. They offer opportunities for teenage actors to delve deeply into the types of age-appropriate, real-life roles and scenarios in which they are most likely to be cast. These include the everyday roles of sons, daughters, older and younger siblings, high school athletes, after-school employees, and other true-to-life characters.

The scripts are clean, gender-neutral, and written in an informal, conversational style that encourages and facilitates a comfortable connection with your audiences. With all this in mind, I expect that most teenagers will also find these monologues relatively easy to memorize.

A monologue of between one hundred fifty to one hundred sixty words in length roughly equates to one minute of performance time on stage or screen. Some of the monologues in this collection are slightly longer – one hundred eighty to one hundred ninety words – but still fit the one-minute requirement when we take into account the natural differences in pacing, tempo, dialect, and speech among performers.

My two previous collections of monologues, **Monologues for Teens** and **Monologues for Kids and Tweens**, included one-minute monologues along with a variety of longer pieces – one to two minutes in length. Those longer pieces are appropriate for advanced students and for those times when a longer monologue may be requested. With this book, however, all one hundred monologues fall into the one-minute category. There is a wide variety of choices. I am certain that with focus, diligent study, and practice, you will find a one-minute monologue here that is a good match for your unique personality, temperament, and skill set – and will serve you well in auditions and performance.

I believe there are greater opportunities available for young people today than ever before in the entertainment industry. I sincerely hope you will find the monologues in this book useful and enjoyable in helping you to reach towards, accomplish, and exceed every one of your show business goals, dreams, and aspirations. I hope you will learn to appreciate, savor, and enjoy every new step forward in your personal actor journey. You can do it. I believe in you and look forward to your great and many successes.

Mike Kimmel
Los Angeles, California

The Opposite of Thank You

Thank you for all that you do and thank you for all that you don't do. Because what you don't do is equally important as what you do. In fact, sometimes it's even more important than what you do daily ... all those good deeds that other people like to thank you for.

So I guess what I'm talking about is the opposite of thank you. It's thank you in reverse.

Thank you for your acts of omission. Thank you for those things you don't do. Thank you for all the trouble you don't cause. Thank you for all the rules you don't break. Thank you for the feelings you don't hurt. Thank you for the disrespectful comments you don't make. Thank you for not rolling your eyes at me while I'm thanking you.

Thank you for all the negative qualities I've never seen in you. Thank you for not being selfish, dishonest, mean-spirited, or cold-hearted.

So thank you from the bottom of my heart for all that you do. And much, much more importantly, thank you for all that you don't do.

1

Now is the Hour

No time to wait ... or waste. Today is the day. Now is the hour. This very day – today – is the tomorrow we all talked about yesterday. Today is the tomorrow we all promised ourselves yesterday.

Remember? Today is the tomorrow you were going to use to get caught up. To start that term paper for English. To finish your science project. To clean your room. To hit the gym.

Et cetera. Et cetera. Ad infinitum.

So roll up your sleeves. Gather your forces. Get your head up out of your shoulders. Stand tall. Stand proud. Take a stand. They say you've gotta stand for something in this world ... or you'll fall for anything. So stand up for today. Today may be the very best day of your life

The best time to plant a tree was twenty years ago. The second best time is now. Right now. Remember – now is the hour. There's no such thing as tomorrow. Because today is the tomorrow we all promised ourselves yesterday.

Yesterday, Today, and Tomorrow

Did you drive here? Is your windshield big or small? Right. It's big. How about your rear view mirror? Big or small? Correct. That's small. For a very good reason.

Where you're going is much more important than where you've been.

Don't let your past define you. Don't let yesterday use up too much of today. Because yesterday is history. Tomorrow is a mystery. But today is a gift. That's why they call it the present.

We've gotta get past our past. Even if you experienced something very bad in your life. Remember, it's not who you are. It's not what you deserved. It's just something that happened. It's over and done. We gotta get a ladder and get over it.

Gotta move forward. Don't trip over something that's way behind you. And don't allow yourself to become a prisoner of your past. Because that bad experience – or even that terrible past experience – was only a life lesson. It was never meant to be your life sentence.

Do They Like Me?

I was extremely shy when I was little. Introverted. Maybe you can relate. Zero self- confidence. I would walk into a room and wonder if people liked me. Now it's different. Now I walk into a room and wonder if I like any of them.

Much better attitude. Because now I don't worry about the haters. There will always be critics and haters. There's never been a shortage. People who feel threatened by your strength, confidence, and peace of mind will always try to put you down, tear you down, and push you around. Always remember that's a reflection of their own weakness. It's all about them, and has nothing whatsoever to do with you.

When someone tells me I can't do something … I do it twice and take pictures. I post 'em on Instagram too.

And when life hands me lemons, I don't make lemonade. I make chocolate chip cookies … and leave the critics and haters scratching their heads. Wondering how I did it.

Always remember … you are in charge of how you feel. And no one can make you feel inferior without your consent.

Boom. Done.

Approve of Yourself

Here's a news flash. Not everyone is going to like you. Some people will talk to you in their free time, and some people will free up their time to talk to you. Pay attention. Learn to recognize the difference.

This is true in your friendships. And in dating too. And don't get caught up in what people look like, either. Because some day, those good looks will fade and you'll be stuck with that horrible personality. So you can't always trust what you see. Salt looks just like sugar.

Seriously, one day we'll all meet the right person. Someone who won't pay attention to anyone's gossip … or what the haters have to say. One day we're gonna meet the people who don't care about our past because they want to become part of our future.

You like that? Yeah, me too.

But meanwhile, don't sit around waiting for someone to approve of you. Disapprove of other people's approval. Learn to approve of yourself. My Uncle Sammy says it best. "Go where you're celebrated, not tolerated."

Be Yourself

I'll tell you, there are some days when I just amaze myself. And then ... there's other days ... when I'll spend an hour looking for my phone before I realize I'm holding it in my hand.

Funny, right? Also true. I guess that makes me a study in contrasts. An exception that makes the rule.

Yep. For as long as I can remember, I never quite fit in. I was never a joiner, either. And that's okay.

Guess that makes me the black sheep in the family. They say I'm different. Not everyone understands me. That's okay too. Just because my path is different doesn't mean I'm lost.

Because I've learned you've got to be comfortable in your own skin. You've got to learn to be yourself. Everyone else is already taken. Never apologize for being you – or for walking boldly in your very own path. Be an individualist ... and an individual.

They say those who fly solo ... always have the strongest wings. Always be yourself ... and always be true to you.

Trust Your Instincts

Trust your instincts. Trust your gut. Trust that beautiful little voice that speaks to you … and always seems to give you the right answer. That little voice speaks to all of us, my friends. And it tells us what we already know deep down is right and true.

My brain has no heart. My heart has no brain. That's why when I speak my mind honestly, I seem heartless. And when I speak deeply from the heart, I appear thoughtless.

That's a conundrum. I get it.

But that's why I always trust my instincts. I've taught myself to always trust my gut. I rely upon that still, small voice from somewhere deep down inside. That's the voice of truth. Maybe that's what they call the conscience.

I trust it. Because my brain can sometimes be fooled and my heart can act like an idiot, but my gut never learned how to tell me a lie.

The Secret of Self-Improvement

Did you ever have an idea about something you want to do? Something you think you should do? But then you talk yourself out of it?

Well, you can talk yourself into it just as easily. You can talk yourself into it instead.

You can. And you should. And if you start, you will. Don't decrease your goal. Increase your effort. And baby steps are okay. The important thing is to get started. Get yourself into action.

"Oh, but I tried everything."

Not true. If you tried everything, you'd accomplish what you were trying to do. You'd finish your homework. You'd ace that test. You'd be a better student. You'd be a better athlete. You'd be in better shape. You'd be a better son, daughter, brother, sister. You'd be a better friend too, believe it or not.

You'd be better at everything. Because opportunities to get better are everywhere. We have access to so much information. To help us get better. And we can. And we should. And we must.

Because baby steps are okay. And better is not something you wish for. Better is something you become.

Taming Our Tongues

Here's a little challenge for you. Learn how to tame your tongue.

When you're having a bad day – a really bad day – try and treat the world better than it's treating you.

Because life is complicated. So we gotta have patience with people. Most people are struggling with all kinds of stressful messes in their lives. Have patience. Trust me, a moment of patience in a moment of anger saves you a million moments of regret.

It's easy to blow up and lose your temper. Too easy. Any old jerk can do that. Doesn't take any special skill or talent to get angry. Anger is the easiest emotion. But we can do better than that. We can set higher standards for ourselves.

We can become the best versions of ourselves. If we try hard, we can even become the people our dogs think we are.

Have patience … and don't complain, either. Think before you talk. Some people say any old thing that pops into their heads. Some people need speed bumps between their brains and their mouths. Don't be like that. Tame your tongue.

Because a smart person knows what to say. But a wise person knows whether or not to say it.

Great-Grandfather's Jacket

I never met my great-grandfather. My dad's grandpa. Actually, Dad never met him either. But I grew up hearing stories about him. My dad's stories about life in the old country. Before his family emigrated to America.

My great-grandfather lived in a country where people didn't have the freedoms we take for granted here. Freedom of speech, freedom to petition the government, freedom of religion.

Great-grandfather had the wrong religion and the wrong politics. That's why the soldiers came to take him away.

He wanted to get his jacket … but one soldier took out his pistol and said, "You don't need your jacket." They put my great-grandfather on the truck and took him away. Nobody ever saw him again.

My father's parents came here for a better life. Freedom. Freedom of speech. Freedom of the press. Freedom from unlawful search and seizure. Freedom of religion. All the freedoms we take for granted.

I never met my great-grandfather. But they named me after him. And I think about him every time I put on my jacket … and nobody points a gun and tells me I'm not allowed to do it.

Frame of Reference

I was waiting in line for ice cream at my favorite place. And waiting and waiting and waiting. I was starting to get a little impatient, to tell you the truth. I'm usually not that way. But I definitely felt a little bit of grumpiness and agitation starting to bubble up from beneath the surface.

Then I remembered stories my grandmother used to tell me. How she waited in line for five hours to buy coffee during the Great Depression. And how my grandfather lived in a DP camp after the war ... and waited three years for his opportunity to come to America.

I know, right? Kinda makes my little impatient attitude sound childish. Kinda puts everything in perspective. Boo hoo. Poor me. Waiting in line ten minutes too long to buy some over-priced, small-portioned gourmet ice cream that I shouldn't be eating anyway.

So keep things in perspective. Maintain your frame of reference. Keep a good attitude today. And remember how fortunate we are to even have the freedom to be impatient ... and complain about all the stupid, moronic, insignificant, annoying little things we complain about all day long.

Winners and Losers

Let me tell you what I've observed about winners and losers. Winners think big. Losers think small. Winners think about getting bigger. Losers think about how to protect themselves from getting smaller.

If you want to go big, stop thinking small. That means get rid of jealousy, pettiness, anger, and unbelief. Stop comparing yourself with others.

Losers always focus on people who are winning. Winners only focus on winning more.

One thing all winners have in common is that they look forward enthusiastically to all the good things the future holds in store. And that means they don't waste precious minutes *today* beating themselves up over mistakes they made yesterday.

Remember, you can't accept what's in front of you until you let go of what's behind you. And if you don't leave your past mistakes back there in the dust ... where they belong ... they will seek to destroy all the promises of your new, improved future.

My advice is simple. Live for what today has to offer, not for what yesterday has taken away.

The 85 Percent Rule

I have a theory. Maybe you'll help me prove it. We're all doing better than we think we are. Agree or disagree?

You may be surprised to hear this. But at any given time, most of the things in our lives are going … reasonably well.

Not perfect. Maybe a couple of things are out of order. But most everything else is pretty much okay.

I'm estimating … about 85 percent. Roughly 85 percent of things in our lives are going well at any given time. I'd say that's pretty good. But what do most people talk about? What do most people focus on? Not the 85 percent. The 15 percent that's not so hot. The 15 percent that's maybe all messed up. The problem areas. People love to talk about their problems. I get that. Totally get it.

But … I don't participate.

I'm not one of those people. I want to be different. I've got a few problem areas too, but I'm aiming higher. I'm focusing on everything that's good in my life. I'm focusing on my own, personal 85 percent of perfect.

Grandfather's Gift

Ilost my pencil. Someone took it from my desk at school. I had this beautiful cobalt blue pencil … with a retractable lead. Like architects and draftsmen use for technical drawings and blueprints. It wrote so nice and smooth. Yeah, I know. This might not mean a lot to you, but it meant a lot to me.

That was the last gift my grandpa ever gave me … in a beautiful blue case. Don't know if it was expensive … but it was absolutely priceless to me.

My grandfather's not around anymore. But I remember all his advice … and the blessing he spoke over my life when I opened his gift at my birthday party all those years ago.

Grandpa said, "Use this pencil to write yourself a beautiful life adventure. Write your own life story … instead of living the story the rest of the world plans out for you. I wish you blue skies and green lights on your journey … and maybe you'll remember your old grandpa from time to time while you're writing your story down."

I'm writing it down, Grandpa. I'm writing it down. And I'm remembering you every day in that story.

Grandma Likes to Walk

My grandmother likes to walk. She walks all the way to the store. Walks back. Walks to her volunteer job. And she takes long walks all around the neighborhood. That might not sound like the best exercise to us ... but for an older person it's still pretty good.

But Grandma wasn't always a grandma. Once upon a time, she was a beautiful young girl ... and a terrific athlete ... a world class athlete.

Grandma has an old silver medal in a wooden box on her coffee table to prove it. From the 1952 Olympics in Helsinki, Finland. My grandmother was just a teenager ... when she left home for the first time ... left the country ... and came back with that gorgeous silver medal.

Nowadays, Grandma's consistent with her walking. Does it every day. Sometimes twice a day. She says our bodies are the houses we were given to live in when we were born. And if we don't take good care of them ... we'll get kicked out of our houses.

And then where are we gonna live?

The Convenience Store

Do you ever shop at a convenience store? You know the kind of store I'm talking about. They have a little bit of this, a little bit of that. People pop in to buy milk, or cigarettes, or a soda when they're on the run.

But then people also stop there on the weekends for beer … and lottery tickets … because it's convenient! And that kinda … makes the lines real long.

They also have an ATM. That's convenient … if you don't have cash … just a card. But they add a pretty hefty fee. What they call a convenience fee. And that's not so convenient.

Then I also noticed the prices … on everything … are much higher than our regular store.

And they have some … characters there too. Wild characters. There's always a … shady character or two hanging around the parking lot. Asking for money … making disgusting comments when a pretty girl walks by. And that's definitely not convenient, either.

So the more I think about it … the more I start to realize … there's nothing more inconvenient than shopping at a convenience store.

Adult Beverages

I got invited to a party Saturday night. That new kid at school is throwing it. His parents are gonna be away all weekend. So he's having something called an Adult Beverage Party.

I never even heard of that before. This kid says the idea is to serve all kinds of mixed drinks. Not just beer, but hard liquor. The hard stuff, the serious stuff, as he describes it.

Count me out. I don't want to go to a party like that. Correct me if I'm wrong, but I believe I may have heard something … somewhere … about underage drinking being … oh, what's the word?

Illegal! Yeah, that's it! Illegal!

Think I've also heard lots of stories about adults guzzling down too many of those tempting adult beverages … wrapping their adult cars around adult trees … landing themselves in adult jail cells … adult emergency rooms … maybe even the adult morgue.

So adult beverages don't sound very adult at all. And that party sounds pretty childish if you ask me. Think I'll stick to teenage fun and games instead.

17

Nobody's Perfect

Nobody's perfect. Have you heard that one before? They're the two most disgusting words in the English language. Or any language.

"Nobody's perfect" is a convenient catch-phrase. People say it to let themselves off the hook. To justify being lazy … to explain themselves for not doing their best. Never even trying to do their best.

There's no shortage of those people. They're everywhere. Nobody's perfect, so why even try? Why knock yourself out?

But this highly imperfect world we were thrown into needs more people who are perfectionists. There's enough of the other type … more than enough people who are happy to slap any old thing together just to get the job done.

We have enough im-perfectionists in the world already. We don't need more of them. We've got that covered. Got that category filled to overflowing.

If you want to stand out … always do your best. Go for that Number One Spot.

And if the odds are one in a million … be the one.

A Three-Legged Dog

I saw a three-legged dog today. Little dog. Like a terrier or something. Missing one of his front legs.

Made me wonder how he got like that. Was he born that way or did something happen?

Not that it matters. Because I watched him for a long time. And he seemed to be getting around pretty well on his own three legs. The ones he has. Not worrying about the one he doesn't have. Not missing the one he's missing! Making the most of all he has left.

That made me think.

This little dog's getting along just fine. He may not have all his limbs, but he's making the most of what he does have. Making the best of an imperfect situation.

A three-legged dog made me think today. More importantly, he made me thank. This dog made me stop and be grateful for all the good things in my life. And made me think long and hard about how to make the most of everything I've got going for me … and against me. How can I make the very best of every imperfect situation in my own life?

19

Thin on Top

My father's going a little thin on top. Don't worry. He's pretty thick everywhere else. Just thin on top. He told me he started losing his hair early ... when he was just a little bit older than I am now.

In his high school yearbook, he was voted most likely to recede. And that prediction eventually came true. His forehead turned into a five-head. So we gotta be careful what we let people speak out over us.

Dad wears a hat ... usually a baseball cap to cover up. The poor man's toupee, he calls it. Gotta be careful what we speak out over ourselves too, though. But that's okay. Dad's got a sense of humor about it. My father says he always wore hats ... even back in high school.

And all his life, people told him, "If you keep wearing a hat, you're gonna go bald."

Dad said, "If I keep wearing a hat, nobody's gonna know."

The Swimsuit

My mom and dad are going on a second honeymoon. Isn't that cool? My parents are awesome. They're excited about this vacation. Like two high school kids going on their first date. I'm proud of them.

So Mom went shopping for a new swimsuit. Took me with her for a second opinion. My mom's kinda sensitive. She looks pretty good in a bathing suit. But she thinks she's too heavy. A lot of grown-ups are sensitive that way.

She tries one on. And ... it was not a success. Just didn't look nice on her. She saw me make a face. Mom said, "Really? That bad?"

I didn't want to hurt her feelings. So I didn't answer.

Then the saleslady said, "Well ... the lighting in this room is not very flattering."

So my mom said, "I'm going to the beach. Do you think the sun will be any dimmer?"

Funny, right? That was a great answer. My mother's not a supermodel, but she's super smart, super cool, and super funny.

And I think that's much more important than how she looks in a bathing suit.

The Map Book

I got lost yesterday. Not lost outside, but lost inside. I got lost in a book. My favorite place to lose myself. Inside a book inside the library.

The weird thing is … it was a big, dusty old book of maps. Right. Maps.

My baby sister says they don't even have a name for that one. But I couldn't help myself. I started looking at one of the maps … a map of a faraway city … and remembered that's where my uncle used to live. I never went there … but always wanted to. Then … all of a sudden, I wished real hard that I could visit.

And I started thinking … maybe there's someone living in that faraway city … someone my age … looking at a map of my faraway city. The place where I live now. And maybe that person is wishing they could visit my city. Just like I'm wishing I could visit theirs.

Maybe we're connected somehow. Maybe not. Maybe it's just a strange idea. But it's an idea that started from a big, dusty old book of maps. That's gotta count for something.

Green Thumb

My Uncle Charlie has a green thumb. That means he spends a lot of time in the garden. Growing plants and flowers. Even some vegetables.

My uncle was in the military years back. Special forces. He hardly ever talks about it, though. I guess he saw some pretty bad stuff. Maybe even did some pretty bad stuff.

Said he's seen enough things torn down, blown up, and destroyed in his lifetime. Had enough of that mess. Now he wants to build stuff back up. That's why he's gardening, raising plants, flowers, food.

Maybe even raising himself up. Growing a new version of him. A new Uncle Charlie. Cultivating new aspects to his personality. Totally reinventing himself.

I bet a lot of grown-ups think they can't ever change. But that's not true. My Uncle Charlie proves it's never too late to start again. He says we should never let yesterday use up too much of today. And I'm really proud of him for that. And I'm proud of him for turning his life around, inspiring me, and having an awesome attitude while he's doing it too.

The Surge Protector

I was doing my homework at the computer. And I looked down at the surge protector. You know … that power strip thingy you plug the computer into … just in case there's … any interruption … any drama … with your electricity.

That surge protector protects the computer … protects all the important, valuable stuff. So your computer doesn't "lose it." Makes sure it doesn't "go off" when some unexpected problem pops up.

I started thinking … I wish they had one of those for people. Because I know people who need a surge protector. They need to protect themselves to make sure they don't get disconnected from their source of power. There's way too many distractions out there.

So stay strong. Stay plugged in to your power source. Stay connected to whatever gives you strength, whatever inspires you … whatever it is that feeds your soul. Don't let anything – or anybody – interrupt you, or stop you from completing your goal, accomplishing your mission, and fulfilling your destiny on this beautiful Earth.

Remember … you stay plugged in.

My Best Friend's Charger

I got a little stuck yesterday. Sometimes we all do. I was in school and my phone started shutting off. Never happened before. I think the battery might be going bad. Maybe something else.

I shut it off and on a couple of times to reset. Nothing. No good.

So I thought maybe I'd let it charge up a while. Worth a try, right? I forgot my charger at home, though, so I got one from my friend Jodie.

Okay. So far, so good. But I plug in and a message screen pops up: "This device may not be supported."

Wow. Another wall. I started getting kinda anxious. It's funny, right? Funny how much we rely on our phones. Can't live without 'em, right?

And maybe my phone is ... a device ... too. An electronic device to help me cope. A device to hide from the world, maybe? Maybe I'm overthinking. But so many of my friends are doing the opposite ... under-thinking.

Maybe I'm really using my phone itself as a device ... to check out ... and hide from the world.

But ... this device may not be supported.

Silent Mode

W hy is silent mode so loud? I put my phone on silent mode – and face down – when I'm in the library. And then it started ringing, and jumping, and buzzing all over the place.

What is up with that, anyway?

It's so loud ... even when it's supposed to be silent!

But then again, I wonder why people are so loud too – even when they're supposed to be quiet and well-behaved. Some people just talk, talk, talk all the time. Even in the library.

And then they're buzzing around like my silent mode cell phone. Bopping all over the place with all that nervous energy. Talking with their friends, sharpening pencils, texting, tapping tables.

Sometimes I wish there was a little switch on the side to put some of these talkers, tappers, and texters on silent mode too.

Because when you get right down to it, people nowadays have become prisoners of their phones. That's why they call them "cell" phones.

The Digital Appendage

Do you notice anything different? About me, I mean. Something missing that most people my age generally have with them ... but I don't have.

No? Okay, I'll give you a hint. There's no blinking, beeping, flashing digital appendage at the end of my arm.

Translation: no cell phone in my hand.

Don't have it. Don't need it. Don't want it.

I think a cell phone is nothing but a great big distraction machine. People are always playing on it and never paying attention to the outside world around them.

It's like a form of mass hypnosis in my school. Everybody's walking around hypnotized ... like digitized zombies ... and nobody ever talks about it. Goofiest thing I ever saw in my whole life.

Cell phones are manipulating people's actions and their minds. Mind control, that's what it is. And pretty soon people won't even have enough mind left for anyone to want to control.

Count me out. I'm not participating. There's one person who's allowed to think inside my head, ladies and gentlemen. And that's me.

Compatibility Check

Are you a techie? A technology geek? Or are you not? Mac or PC? Maybe I'm a Mac and you're a PC ... or you're a Mac and I'm a PC ...

Are we ... compatible? Because compatibility is of utmost importance ... if two are ever going to move forward. And network together as one. Gotta verify our compatibility index. See if we can merge.

Nowadays that's not always possible ... because of all the available options. Everybody's trying to advance themselves. Everybody wants to upgrade.

But sometimes our thinking gets stuck. It freezes up. And we gotta reboot.

But are we even on the same interface? Are you gonna download when I want to upload? Or am I gonna download when you try to upload? These are very important considerations.

Can we even be together? Can we coexist? Because if we're to make any kind of progress at all, we gotta make sure we're communicating. We gotta make sure we are always ... in synch.

The Computer Lab

Every Tuesday afternoon my teacher takes the class to the computer room. Probably a good idea. I guess they want to break up the monotony.

But what about the monotony of the computer lab? Honestly, we do some good exercises ... reading comprehension ... grammar review ... vocabulary builder. But we waste so much time getting to those good exercises -- that it's not even worth it! I don't think it is. Just my opinion ...

We're only there for one hour, but our teacher spends half that time circulating among the students ... helping everybody log in!

Half my classmates can't remember their passwords or even their user names. Know what? They sure don't have any trouble remembering the password to unlock their phones. That's for sure.

So what the heck is the issue with remembering something for our schoolwork?

I've got an idea. How about linking our schoolwork to everybody's social media platform of choice? Hmmm? You like that? I like it too.

Let's see how many "likes" I can get with that one ...

Wisdom Through Experience

You are looking at a highly intelligent human being. Super smart. Maybe not the smartest you've ever met, but I'm the smartest I've ever been. I stand before you today with wisdom achieved through experience and analysis. Sometimes very painful analysis ... of my own past mistakes.

Yes, I've made mistakes.

But today, I am strong because I've been weak. Today, I am fearless because I've been scared. Today, I am wise because I've made some pretty foolish choices in my past.

So ... I want to encourage you today ... no matter what your personal history has been.

Take action. I firmly believe that all of us know what we need to do today to make tomorrow a little bit better for ourselves. Don't be afraid of making mistakes. Einstein said the only person who doesn't make mistakes is a person who doesn't do anything.

Be decisive. Make decisions, right or wrong. We gain wisdom through experience. Because the long, winding road of life is paved with flat squirrels who could never decide which way to go.

Kinda Blah

Did you ever just feel kinda blah? Not horrible. Not terrible. Not bad enough to stay home from school or go to the doctor.

Just a little foggy. Just a little cloudy. Just feeling kinda ... blah.

I think we all get like that. But what should we do when we get like that? I'll tell you what I do ... since you asked so nice. I look at my list of things to do for the day, and I say, "No way." If I don't feel my best, I can't do my best.

But you can do a little. Maybe you can't do everything, but you can do something. A little bit of something is better than a whole lot of nothing. So get up and do something when you're feeling kinda blah. It'll help you feel ... kinda not so blah.

Hope you were paying attention. Because I'm not gonna repeat all this. I would if I could, but I can't so I won't.

Because ... to tell you the truth ... I'm feeling kinda ... blah.

Overcoming Doom and Gloom

I have a complaint about one of my teachers. He's always complaining. He complains about everything. He complains about the school administration. He complains about the curriculum. He even complains about his students. Yeah, that's right, he complains to us about us!

Think about it, though. That's probably not an ideal way to connect with your students – or anyone. Besides, how many people enjoy listening to someone's complaints? Zero.

Because everybody knows we get what we focus on. If we talk about our problems, we'll draw more problems to us. If we're always complaining, we'll always have more and more to complain about. Gotta get more positive instead.

Sounds good, right? But how do we create that additional optimism? Bring a fresh, new positivity into our lives if it's not already there? Answer: Find a way. It's different for everyone. Find a way even when it's difficult. Find a way even when there is no way.

Because it's up to you. It's what you do in the dark that always brings you back into the light.

Twitchy McItchy

We got a kid in our class who can't keep still. He's always squirming back and forth. Can't sit still. Can't even stand still.

Always twitching. Twitching all over the place. Really twitchy. We call him Twitchy McItchy.

I don't know why he is the way he is, but most of my classmates get really annoyed with him. I think he even gets annoyed with himself sometimes. Because he doesn't have the capacity to sit still. And that's a problem. People need to be able to calm down and keep still so they can focus and concentrate on what's going on in class. But Twitchy McItchy can't do that. He's like a BB bouncing around inside a soda can. Always moving but never getting anywhere.

That's the problem with a lot of people nowadays. They're busy, but not productive. They're moving, but not moving forward. Don't let that happen to you. Don't be like that. Make sure you stay active. And never mistake twitchy activity for real progress.

More Money

I've got this great after-school job. Great. But the job would be perfect if they paid a little better. So I asked my supervisors for a raise in pay. They said no. So I asked, "Okay, how about the same money … just paid more frequently?" No.

My dad says not to worry about money. Plenty of time for that when I get older. Dad says people spend money they don't have, to buy things they don't need, to impress people they don't like.

Okay. Point well taken.

But is it really so wrong to want more money? To put a few more jingles in my pocket? More than when I started this job? Don't think of it as capitalism. Think of it as change … evolution.

Because if nothing ever changed, the world would have no butterflies, right?

That's how we gotta go through life. Thinking outside the box and seeing the big picture. With an upbeat attitude and an optimistic outlook. And a little more money in our pockets sure wouldn't hurt.

You follow me? Don't follow me. I'll call the cops.

Fifty Percent of Something

I read this story about Elvis Presley. One of the greatest singers of all time. Way before my time, but I love his music.

But this wasn't a story about his singing. It was a story about his manager. His relationship – his business relationship – with his manager, Colonel Parker. Everybody just called him the Colonel.

Apparently, Elvis used to give fifty percent of the money he earned to the Colonel.

That's a lot. Most singers and actors give their managers ten percent. Maybe fifteen.

But Elvis said he wanted to give the Colonel more incentive to find jobs for him. Good jobs. Elvis would rather have fifty percent of millions of dollars than ninety percent of thousands of dollars. And that made a whole lot of sense to me.

That sounded like an outside the box way of thinking about business.

Elvis was giving away a bigger piece of the pie ... but the Colonel was bringing a much bigger pie into that kitchen. Good arrangement, because that creates more pie for everyone. And I am always in favor of more pie. And more Elvis.

The Coming Attractions

I was at the movies last weekend. Have you noticed anything funny at the movies lately? Not ha-ha funny … weird funny?

I'm talking about the coming attractions. So many!

I got to the theater right on time. But the coming attractions went on and on forever. I got really irritated. Perhaps you've figured that out already. I got so annoyed, I started timing them. Would you believe the coming attractions went on … and on … for twenty minutes. Twenty minutes! Nearly one third the length of the movie I paid for!

That's way too long. The mathematics do not calculate out correctly. The old time film director Cecil B. DeMille said, "The first star of a motion picture should be its story."

Exactly. The story is the star. Not the story of the *other* movies playing there next week and the week after.

So treat your audience better, Mr. Theater Manager. We paid to see a movie … not to be tantalized with all the movies you want us to see next.

Okay. I'm officially done now. Can we please move on? Start the movie.

A Rant on Vending Machines

Lemme get this straight. Facial recognition software can pick a wanted criminal out of a crowd, but the vending machine at school can't recognize a dollar bill with a bent down corner?

Why can't we upload better ... presidential facial recognition software onto our vending machines? A dollar bill has a picture of George Washington on it. George Washington? Everybody knows what he looks like, right? So what the heck's the problem?

I thought we had good, solid, top of the line technology to work with. Apparently not. Because my dollar bill was rejected seventy-two times today by that vending machine at school. And those M&Ms ... the ones with my name on them ... are not melting in my mouth as I'd hoped they would be right now. So apparently, we are still quite technologically challenged here on Planet Earth.

Maybe we need alien technology. Like they had in Roswell, New Mexico.

Alien technology? Nah. Not too likely. Aliens probably fly right past our planet in their spaceships and lock their big, shiny, round doors.

Making Plans

I've got a friend who is very consistent. Consistently late. Every time we're supposed to get together – to study, go to the mall, or just grab a burger – my friend Alex is consistently twenty minutes late.

So I devised a plan. I started showing up late too. I tried that several times. Bingo. We both started arriving at the exact same time. Worked like magic. Perfect synchronicity.

Because people are not machines. And not everybody's going to act the way we would like them to act. You can't force people to become mirror images of yourself. You can't put a steering wheel to someone's back and make them go where you want them to … or behave the way you want them to.

But … what you can do … is figure out every different person's different way of operating. You do that by observing their actions. Look at what people do, not what they say. And then you make adjustments based on their actions.

That's how you achieve … perfect synchronicity in making plans with people. Well, at least … that's how you aim for it, anyway.

Take the Best. Leave the Rest.

At what point do you say, "I quit?" At what point do you say "No more?" At what point do you say "I surrender?" Those are the hard questions I frequently pose to myself ... when I'm waiting for a friend. And waiting ... and waiting ... and waiting.

Because sometimes my friends are not on time. And sometimes I get annoyed. And sometimes ... I have to stop myself before I get angry and say something I might regret later. Because people are not always going to behave the way you and I would like them to behave.

Consequently, sometimes I feel like I have to de-escalate myself. That's college talk for "calm down." That's when I say to myself, "Okay, Self. Take the best. Leave the rest."

Don't worry about who's late ... or how late. Just appreciate. Appreciate the company of your good friends. And realize how much you'd miss them if you didn't have them for friends in your life any more.

Remember, don't judge. Just appreciate. Take the best. Leave the rest.

Forgiveness

Can I share a secret? A lot of people have a problem with somebody in their lives. From their past. A lot of people have a problem … with forgiveness.

Forgiveness is tough. Because a lot of us have been hurt. Most people have been through a rough time. But you've got to get past it. Get a ladder and get over it. Because forgiveness is important. It's one of the most important qualities a person can develop.

Forgiveness demonstrates refinement. Ghandi said forgiveness is a sign of strength, not weakness. Weak people don't have it in them to forgive. And we don't forgive the other person for their sake. We forgive them for our sake … so we don't have to hold on to all that anger and emotional baggage anymore. Stop carrying around that junk from yesterday.

Forgiveness frees up mental space inside your head. Don't let that negative person or negative situation live rent-free inside your mind for one more day. Because what forgiveness really means … is that you're giving up all hope of a better past.

Leave It Behind You

I'm a pretty good writer. That's what I do best. And I have a friend who's been telling me forever that he wants me to help him write a long paper for extra credit.

I enjoy the writing process. I've assisted quite a few friends and classmates with their essays. But writing this long essay proved a little daunting for my friend – and that's completely understandable. What's not understandable, though, are all the excuses.

Had to work extra hours at his job. Had to watch his little brother. Had to pick his Uncle Charlie up from the airport.

The worst, though, was when he told me he had a bad back. A bad back? I said, "That's okay. You've got a great front. Use what's in front of you, instead of what's behind you. Besides, you write with your hand ... and your head ... not your back. Leave your bad back behind you."

In fact ... leave everything bad behind you ... where it can't trip you up anymore ... where it can never slow you down or hold you back ... ever again.

My Favorite Squirrel

I see him every day. Or her. I'm not exactly sure if he's a him or she's a her. But whatever he is, he's super cute. Comes to my door every morning to say hello. Always puts me in a good mood. Always starts my day with a smile.

My favorite squirrel. Looks just like a dog, but I don't have to walk him.

Or feed him … but, to tell you the truth, I feed him anyway.

Not out of my hand. I know that could be dangerous.. Squirrels look cute, but they could have rabies. Or some other bad stuff I don't want to bring in the house. But I can still feed him outside the house. I'll leave nuts and raisins – all kinds of stuff – outside for him.

He gobbles it up and keeps coming back for more. That makes me feel really good. Guess he likes the food I set out for him.

Or maybe he just likes me. How about that? Maybe I'm his favorite human … just like he's my favorite squirrel.

A Brand New Telescope

I got a telescope for my birthday. Best. Gift. Ever. I took it out of the box and started working with it right away.

I spent the first few nights looking through the telescope at the stars twinkling in the night sky. Trying to identify every constellation. Planets are easy. Just a few of them. Easy to identify.

Then I started thinking ... "Hey ... what if someone out there is looking back at me?"

Maybe some alien kid on another planet got a telescope for his birthday too. And he's scoping out the stars and planets from his side of the universe ... trying to figure it all out too. Trying to find intelligent life.

And how weird would it be if he's looking back at me here on Earth looking up at him ... way up there ... far away on his planet?

Could be embarrassing, right? Good thing I'm wearing a clean T-shirt. Well ... almost clean. Except for that little grease stain I got from putting my new telescope together ...

Black and White Movies

Do you ever watch black and white movies? Those movies from a long, long time ago? That's what I started doing lately.

And, you know what? I'm kinda hooked! Most of the kids in my school won't watch black and white. They say they can't get into those old movies. And I get it. It was hard for me at first too. It was a little uncomfortable. Then, once I started getting more comfortable with the format, it became second nature for me.

Not much different from watching a brand new movie in the theater.

And these movies WERE new in the theater once upon a time. Except that time was many, many years ago. And those fashions and styles were new many years ago too.

And those people in those movies – who were so happy to be acting in a movie – are probably all gone now. And that makes me kinda sad.

Because people are the same all over. All over the world and all through time. In color and in black and white. People are always the same, yesterday, today, and tomorrow. That could have been us in those old movies.

The Other Side of Sunset

My drama teacher recommended a movie. "Sunset Boulevard." Old. Black and white. Classic.

She said, "Watch it and see what you learn about Hollywood." I don't like black and white. But I watched the whole thing ... and now I'm glad I did.

It's the story of an old Hollywood star, Norma Desmond. She sits in her old mansion on Sunset Boulevard ... watching her old movies over and over again. It was sad, but it made me think about people who have great careers out in Hollywood ... and are then forgotten.

I think that's what my teacher wanted us to see. Possibly to discourage us? Well, I'm not easily discouraged. Won't listen to the negative cheerleading team.

So I watched Sunset Boulevard and I was encouraged. I thought about how many people want to act ... but never even try. Because everyone tells them how difficult it is. I like people like Norma Desmond ... who tried and gave it their best.

Because not everyone can be a movie star – like she was – but everyone can put their heart and soul into their acting ... like she did.

That's How I Roll ...

I just don't get it.

These other guys can hurry if they'd like. But I don't see the advantage in ... bringing forth my inner lead foot ... pushin' that pedal hard ... burning up all that gas ... and rushing to get up to that red light ... before the car next to me.

So I say ... let's all just relax ... please. Take a chill pill ... please. Pretty please with sugar on top.

Years ago, people used to take their cars out and go for a nice leisurely drive... just to relax. I think those days are long since past. Long gone. But I would really like to bring them back if I can.

Because I'm looking forward to a lifetime of blue skies and green lights. So when I get to a red light, well ... I suppose that's all just part of the process.

And that's how I roll, brothers and sisters ... down the highways and bi-ways of life.

Red lights ... are just another part of the process.

Optimist? Pessimist? Both? Neither?

A re you an optimist or pessimist? I'm not sure what I am. I think I've been a little bit of each. I can identify with both. I'm equally comfortable on both sides of that spectrum. And that's good. Because this world needs both.

Optimists invented the airplane. Pessimists invented the parachute.

We need both in life. We need the optimists ... the big thinkers ... with the creative ideas to launch us boldly into the future.

At the same time, we need those skeptical sourpusses to help temper that optimism ... and make sure we keep both feet planted on terra firma ... to ensure a safe and effective launch ...and landing. Which is most important?

Both. Neither. All of the above. We need both. The optimist and the pessimist. The plus and the minus. The yin and the yang. The whole is always greater than the sum of its parts.

I guess you'd call that seeing the glass half full ... rather than half empty. And I guess that ... kinda makes me an optimist.

The Audition Trip

We just came back from Los Angeles. My acting teacher took our class on a trip. An audition trip. We met all kinds of show biz people. Agents, casting directors, producers, and directors.

We really learned a lot. Some of my classmates were a little disappointed, though. I think they expected to be "discovered" ... to get some kinda big job right away and be on TV. But I think that's the wrong approach. This was supposed to be a learning trip. Intended to immerse us in the process.

And this process is terrific. But you gotta let it work. You gotta let it simmer. You gotta let yourself experience the process and really learn.

That means roll up your sleeves. That means take classes. That means read books. That means study scripts. That means learn your lines.

And that takes time. I bet the famous actors we see on TV didn't get discovered right away. They probably had to work and work and work for their success. And then work some more.

And ... that's probably what you and I should do too.

The Hall of Fame

I have to tell you about what I call the Hall of Fame. When we were out there in Los Angeles for our audition trip, we visited the coolest place. The Television Academy.

It was so inspiring. The Television Academy is the organization that produces the Emmy Awards. That's like the Oscars – but for the best TV shows – instead of movies.

And they have this beautiful building in North Hollywood with a gorgeous, state of the art theater.

But my favorite part was actually outside the theater. I call it the Hall of Fame. There's statues all around the building. Statues of famous actors from years ago. You can walk around and take your picture with the old time actors, directors, and producers too.

Well ... you can take your picture with their statues, anyway.

We got lots of great pictures. It's an incredible opportunity to make people feel like they're part of history. Part of something special. Part of the TV Academy. Part of the entertainment industry's own, personal Hall of Fame.

It's my personal Hall of Fame too.

Donuts Divided

I work a part time job on weekends. That's not a bad thing. That's a good thing. Matter of fact, they even have donuts at my job sometimes. My favorite food group.

They had 'em this morning. But by the time I clocked in, there were only a couple of half donuts in the box. Donuts that had been sliced in half. Cut down in their prime. That's totally against the rules.

Cutting a donut in half curtails its effectiveness, eliminates its perfect roundness, its unique donut-hood. Chops it off at both ends. Cuts it off in the middle too. Bisecting a donut ruins that donut for all of us ... forever.

Dividing donuts compromises their unique donut-hood. Their special donut-ness. So if there's a box of donuts on the table, there should be no knives anywhere in that room. Nowhere in the vicinity. Can't have 'em. Donuts and knives must forever remain mutually exclusive.

Bifurcating a donut is now – and must forever remain – unacceptable behavior. And that should not just be our guideline. That should always be our rule.

Artificial Sweeteners

I'm not a fan of artificial sweeteners. Actually, I'm not a fan of artificial anything. Artificial colors. Artificial preservatives. Even artificial intelligence.

But especially artificial sweeteners. And I'm not talking about the kind you put in your coffee. I'm talking about the kind other people put in your ear. Sweet nothings people whisper in your ear to talk you into doing stuff. Things they want you to do for them.

Some people will tell you whatever they think you want to hear. They talk so nice and sweet. But they're really being fake. They're not real. They're sprinkling their fake artificial sweeteners all over you.

Don't fall for it. Don't get caught in their trap. That sugary-sweet quicksand trap. People have been playing that game for years. Centuries, even.

That's long enough for people like you and me to figure out how to avoid it. George Washington said it's better to be alone than in bad company. He was right. I've had enough artificial sweetener for a lifetime. And now ... I'm kinda sour on all those kinda sweeteners.

The County Fair

We went to the county fair last weekend. Me, my brother, and my parents. It was pretty fun, I guess. The food was good. They had some nice displays to look at. Some good stuff on sale.

Everything was fine except ... the carnival games.

Right, the carnival games. Yeah, yeah, I know. They're supposed to be fun. Well, okay ... but a lot of things that are supposed to be ... aren't. And a lot of things that are NOT supposed to be ... are.

At these carnival games, they were charging a whole lot of money. And at these carnival games, nobody was actually winning.

It was rigged. Surprise, surprise. A crooked carnival game. Designed for people to lose money. Not a lot of money ... but still. Kinda stinks, right?

But I guess that's a warning sign, a wake-up call. Things are not always what they seem to be in life. There's times in life when we're sure we're gonna win ... and there's times when we need to walk away ... because the game is rigged ... and the odds are one hundred percent stacked against us.

Shaking Hands

What is it about shaking hands? What's up with that? Why do so many people want to shake your hand ... especially during flu season?

And did you ever notice that the people who want to shake hands most ... are the people who look like they haven't washed their hands since the vernal equinox?!

What is this big attraction for hand shaking anyway? It doesn't even mean anything! Just an empty gesture.

Do you know where the custom comes from? Back in the old days, knights in shining armor would extend their right hand as a gesture of peace. To show strangers on the road they're not carrying any weapons ...

But nowadays, we *are* carrying weapons! We're carrying so many germs in those extended hands. Almost as dangerous as those old-time battle swords.

So if you ask me, shaking hands is not only old-fashioned, it also goes against common sense ...

Remember ... you only have one chance to make a good first impression.

And the last thing you ever want to do ... is spread that nasty old-fashioned flu.

Those Were the Days

Those Were the Days. The good old days. Have you ever heard people talk about the good old days? I sure have. My grandpa talks about the good old days all the time. "Those were the days," he says. And my grandma is so funny. She always says, "Remember, dear ... these are the days too."

I love that. These are the days too. These are the good old days.

These are the days we'll look back on sometime in the future ... longingly. Yes. Longingly.

Someday, we're going to look back on all the nice things we'll see and hear and touch and smell and taste today.

And we'll miss them so much. Maybe we'll even miss things we take for granted today. So remember ... these are the days. Today is a day. Today is a really good day to have a really good day.

So, yes, those were the days, Grandpa. Those will always be the days. But these will always be the days too.

Turn Back the Clock

Why do we turn the clock back an hour? And then forward an hour? Is there some strange, mystical reason we have to change our timeframe and then change it right back again six months later?

I could never figure that one out. I think a lot of people can't.

And why do so many adults want to turn back the clock of their lives? My grandpa always says ... "if I had my life to live over again" ...

But he doesn't. He only has his life to live forward – not backwards. Forward from this moment on. My grandpa has a lot of regrets. And that's a wake-up call for young people like us.

Make the most of the time that you've got ... today and every day. And maybe you can help someone else out there do the same. When they start talking about turning back that old tick-tock clock of their own.

My Grandparents' Old Car

My grandparents buy a new car every three years. And they give their old car to one of their grandchildren. My grandparents are pretty amazing.

This year, they gave their old car to my brother Ozzie. Ozzie's a real good driver. Ozzie's a real good student. And Ozzie's a real good brother. What Ozzie's not so good at ... is gratitude.

Mom and Dad asked my brother to write a little thank you note to Grandma and Grandpa for their kindness and generosity. I thought that was a great idea. So did Ozzie. Very gracious ... but Ozzie never actually did it. Not that he didn't want to ... maybe he did ... but he never got around to doing it.

Said it's no biggie because he had good intentions. But if good intentions don't *really* materialize, they do nobody any good. Really. And when someone gives you a car, "thank you" should definitely be *spoken out...* and *written out* ... not just *intended*.

Because when all is said and done, more is always said than done. And well done is always better than well said.

The Power of Feet

My mom always tells me this story. Not a story, exactly, but a poem.

"I had the blues because I had no shoes.
Until one day, upon the street,
I met a man who had no feet."

Short, sweet, and to the point, right? What's this poem about? Simple. Gratitude. Being grateful for what we have ... and not focusing on what we don't have. Especially material things. Material things won't take the place of things we got for free ... and can never be replaced.

How much are your feet worth to you? Would you trade them for a million dollars? How about just one little toe? How much is that worth? Think about how much you would miss that toe if ... you didn't have it anymore. Think about how much you would miss your family ... or your best friend ... or any of the ga-zillion other things we all take for granted.

Try it. Start today. Start appreciating everything you take for granted. Show gratitude every day ... and everywhere you go.

And when you do ... you'll be more appreciated too.

Inside and Outside

There was this story in the paper. About a guy who worked in a school. Older man. Worked there fifty years … just cleaning up.

Cleaning classrooms, bathrooms, hallways. Everything.

Always friendly with the students. Friendly to everybody. One of those rare, wonderful people who just loved his job.

And it showed through on the outside. He was everyone's favorite custodian. Very humble. Drove an old car … wore old clothes … packed his lunch in a paper bag.

This man passed away last month … and left all his money to the school. All of it. Three and a half … million … dollars.

Nobody knew he was a millionaire. Guess it just goes to show. Don't judge people by what's outside. How they look … how they act … or what you think their outside life reflects from the inside.

People are full of surprises. Never what they seem.

Your custodian might be a millionaire. And that rich person in the fancy car may have a few surprises that we can't see.

At least not from the outside … trying to look in.

Your Most Dangerous Adversary

Procrastination is dangerous. Your Most Dangerous Adversary. That may surprise some people, but I'll explain.

Procrastination works against you from the inside out. So you gotta learn to outsmart it. And it's tricky ... like playing a game of chess ...

And like a chess game ... or any other game of strategy ... a little time spent in studying your opponent will benefit you in the long run.

The most important thing for all of us to understand is that when you're trying to beat Procrastination ... what you're actually doing is playing a chess game against yourself. Right. You are your own opponent. You're fighting against yourself ... and that's a dangerous opponent because we know ourselves better than anyone. We know all the little tricks to make us lose focus and delay us from doing the things we most need to do with our time ... and with our lives.

So take time to study yourself honestly. And learn to beat Procrastination from the inside out ... before Your Most Dangerous Adversary has a chance to stop you ... or even slow you down.

Anticipate Every Hole in the Boat

My dad never served in the military. But his friends did. My father has a lot of friends who served in the armed forces. They're different than his civilian friends. That's what Dad always says. They behave differently, he tells me. "A breed apart" is what he calls them.

Example. My dad's friends always hold the door open for ladies. When they're going in a room or getting in the car.

They always hold the door. Dad describes it as "Officer and a Gentleman mindset." Even those who are enlisted men – with no stripes on their sleeves – they still behave like gentlemen.

Okay. Maybe not all of them. Not everybody has those high standards.

One thing they do have in common, though, is this: Preparation. They're always prepared for whatever comes up.

They figure out everything that can go wrong. Then they plan around it. Dad's military buddies say, "Anticipate every hole in the boat."

What a great philosophy to help navigate those rough waters of life. I love it. It works for the military, and it will work for us civilians too. Anticipate every hole in the boat.

And hold the door for a lady. It's just good manners.

Holding Her Purse

My Uncle Jack has a new girlfriend. Had, I should say. They just split ... over something truly stupid. Too bad, because I liked this one. Much better than the last three.

But they went out to a show. Not a movie, but a play ... in the theater. His girlfriend had to use the restroom, but she didn't want to bring her purse inside. It was a really small, tiny, little restroom, apparently. A one-sie.

And my uncle's soon-to-be-ex-girlfriend asked my uncle to kindly hold her purse.

And my uncle – macho man that he is – scored a new low for men everywhere ... and the fine art of chivalry by replying, "Sorry, babe. I don't think we're there yet."

You don't think you're there yet? Well, guess what? You're not gonna get there after that one, Uncle Jack. But, hey, you maintained your precious machismo. I guess that's what's really important. Nobody saw you holding your lady friend's purse in the lobby of that theater.

So congratulations. You win. But let me ask you a question, Uncle Jack... what, exactly, did you win?

A Baker's Dozen

Are you familiar with the term, "a baker's dozen?" It's an interesting concept. The idea is that a professional baker – when baking cookies or muffins, for example – bakes thirteen to a dozen, not just twelve. A baker's dozen is thirteen. The extra one is for the baker. So he can taste it and make sure it's up to his own high quality standards.

It implies a little extra care. A little extra effort. A little extra something the baker puts into his work.

How can you and I do the same? Not with baking, but with our own work? School work, homework, all kinds of work.

How can we learn to look at what we're doing every day and take the time to put in a little extra effort? And make sure we put all that we have into all that we do? So we can be sure everything we do is up to our own high quality standards – that we set for ourselves?

And then … begin to raise our own high quality standards daily? And create our own baker's dozen.

The First Ten Thousand

I'm taking this photography class in school. I've been snapping pictures since I was little, so I figured I'd step up my game ... really kick it up a notch.

And this class has been great. But my work in this class has been ... not so great. My teacher has us thinking about things I never thought about before ... color, composition, texture, perspective. Those are all good things. Except I never really worked on them before.

Maybe I understood some of them – or some aspects – intuitively ... but I never thought about them actively ... or put them into practice before snapping a picture.

Now I do.

And our teacher told us something really interesting ... a quote by a famous old-time French photographer. "Your first ten thousand photographs," he said, "will be your worst."

Whoa. That idea blew me away. Because it means we've got to shoot thousands and thousands of pictures just to start getting it right. And that's just to start ... just to get comfortable.

So ... how long does it take to get really, really good? I'll try to find out.

63

I Know This Place

Iknow this place. I've been here before. Didn't recognize the name or address when they gave me the appointment. But now that I'm here … I know this place. This was my grandfather's favorite restaurant. Not too fancy, but very nice. He used to take me here all the time for spaghetti and meatballs.

Absolutely the best place. Best food. Best service. Best everything. And now … here I am applying for a job. Now they need a part-time waiter. I remember that funny little old man with the fancy, curly moustache who used to be our waiter all those years ago. He was even older than Grandpa, probably. Just creaking along, but still working. Bringing us our food with that great old-school style. Service with a smile. I guess he must be long gone by now too. Like my grandpa's gone.

They're both gone. But, you know what? I'm here. And maybe I'll be here a lot. Maybe every weekend. And maybe people will remember me someday … old school style … service with a smile. Fancy, curly mustache optional.

Future Version of Me

Who's your hero? Do you have one? My hero is me at a future date. The Future, Idealized Version of Me.

So I sat down and had a long talk with the Future Version of Me. I asked, "How are we gonna do this? How are we gonna boost me up to where you already are now? How are we gonna pull off all the things I wanna do with my life? All the things I wanna accomplish? All the things I wanna say and do and be ... Future Version of Me?"

And the Future Version of Me answered. My Future Me said to look past what's just in front of me ... and aim higher, dig deeper, and think more creatively.

Look inward, not outward. Because many people are lost nowadays. Searching. Looking for answers.

Don't look for answers. You yourself are the answer. Walk like it. Talk like it. Plan for it. Become an answer in someone else's world. Then you'll evolve ... grow stronger ... until you finally become the New, Improved, Idealized ... Future Version of You.

Second Guessing

I second-guessed myself today. I had a paper due for English. I said I wouldn't wait till the last minute again. That's why I started working on it way in advance ... so I wouldn't be stressed when it was due.

However, on the day the paper was due ... today ... I started second-guessing myself. I don't know why. I worked so hard on this essay ... it was perfect ... but then I wanted to change the conclusion before handing it in.

So I pulled it up on my laptop real quick ... and changed it around. Then I read it over and loved the new ending. Then ... I read it over again ... and didn't. But ... as I started out the door ... I wasn't so sure ... maybe it was better before ... so I changed it back again. Back to the original way it was before.

So I second-guessed myself ... then I guess I second-guessed the second guess. That's a third guess. All that stress ... second-guess ... no rest ... just to go back to the original version I had before.

Nevermore.

Letter of Recommendation

I asked one of my teachers to write a letter of recommendation for me. I needed it for my college application. It's actually for a special program at the college I'm trying to get into.

I had one recommendation letter already, but I needed two. My guidance counselor wrote the first one and I thought it was pretty good. Nothing fancy, but pretty good. Definitely served its purpose.

Let me explain … I thought the first one was pretty good until I saw the new one my teacher wrote. I picked it up after fifth period today. It was … amazing.

I couldn't even believe all the wonderful things this teacher had to say about me. Her letter was filled with praise. She said I was … responsible … conscientious … creative … inventive … cooperative … ambitious.

I was actually kinda shocked. Is she talking about me?

Apparently so. I never knew she thought that highly of me. But sometimes we have to believe in someone else's belief in us until our own belief kicks in and we start believing in ourselves. And now I finally do. Now I really, really do.

Be Ready on Time

Did you ever have to pick someone up and they're not ready? That happens to me with my friend Pat all the time. Good friend, but I have to drive way outta my way to pick this person up, incidentally.

Which I don't even mind doing. Well ... usually don't mind doing.

What I do mind is driving out of my way to pick my friend up ... and my friend is not ready ... keeps me waiting in the car twenty minutes, and then barely even says thank you for driving all the way out there ... ... then all the way back to my side of town ... where we wanted to end up in the first place. And here I am, providing door-to-door service with a smile.

Okay, maybe just a hint of a smile.

It's funny. Because I probably wouldn't mind so much if I was appreciated a little bit more ... or disrespected a little bit less.

So here's my advice. Be ready on time. And maybe even say thank you once in a while ...

The Mother of Invention

Necessity is the mother of invention. Have you heard that? My parents say it all the time.

But if necessity is the mother of invention, then why is so much unnecessary stuff invented?

All this unnecessary stuff. More stuff. New stuff. Better stuff. Improved stuff. Who needs it?

It's mass hypnosis. We've all fallen for it at one time or another. Bigger TV. New phone. New car. New platform for streaming all those movies ... that we already don't have enough time to watch.

All unnecessary distractions to keep people busy ... and keep people buying. Busy, busy, busy. Buying, buying, buying. All this stuff we don't need and won't use.

Well, I've invented the solution. Self-determination. I'm no longer participating. Going old school. No tablet. No cell phone. Going to school today ... the old-fashioned way. Pencil, notebook, eraser. Done.

I am now immune to the invention of ... the mountains of stuff created to distract and hypnotize me.

Don't be impressed. Because necessity really is the mother of invention. And I invented this creative solution for myself ... because it finally became necessary.

The Weeds

Did you ever do any gardening work? I did. Cut grass for all the neighbors when I was in middle school.

It's hard work. And the hardest part is weeding. Pulling out weeds. Because weeds pop up all over the garden. Everywhere.

They don't need to be watered. They don't need to be fertilized. They don't need to be cultivated. They just pop up on their own. Kinda like other problems in our lives. They just show up on our doorstep. Nobody invited them. We didn't seek them out.

Problems, difficulties, stresses – just like weeds – are always available.

Weeds don't need any encouragement to grow. They can grow right through concrete. What's bad is always available. And what's good is also always available. But what's good needs encouragement to grow. What's good needs to be watered, nurtured, and cultivated.

Think about that next time weeds show up in your garden. We have to do more than just rip them out. Trust me. We have to dig down deep and encourage what's good in the world to step forward and show up in their place.

Purge Your List

Evaluate the people and situations in your life. Then promote, demote or terminate them as you see fit.

After all, you're the president and CEO of your own life. You're the big dog. You're the top banana. You're the ultimate decision maker.

So never let anyone put you down, pull you down, or push you around.

Stop putting up with bad behavior. Stop waiting for someone to change.

Don't ask yourself why a clown keeps acting like a clown. Ask yourself why you keep going to the circus.

Stop wishing for a light at the end of the tunnel … and shine your own light on that problem situation and those problem people yourself.

And it's not going to be easy to do. It's not always easy to purge your list. But you've gotta get started. Get into action and watch what happens. Sometimes even the smallest step in the right direction is the most important step you can ever take. And baby steps are okay too. So tip-toe if you must, but do your best to take that first step today, not tomorrow.

Flowers for Someone Special

I bought flowers for someone special today. Somebody I really like. Friends told me not to. Too much too soon. Putting my heart out there. Never a good idea.

But I wanted to show this person I like them. And I liked them for a really long time. Just never had the courage to say anything. Until now … and that's the reason for the invitation. And the flowers.

I couldn't wait to see the expression on my special someone's face. So excited. Wore my best outfit. Made sure it was pressed too. I never do that.

I could hardly wait. But I had to wait. Someone special was late. Thirty minutes. No call, no text. Sixty minutes. Then ninety. Finally, I faced the facts. Stood up. All dressed up, nowhere to go.

As I was leaving, I saw an older lady. She showed up to meet her special someone too. I gave her my flowers … to give to her date. Now at least they won't go to waste. So … you see? I didn't lie. I bought flowers for someone special today. Someone special who I never even met.

Two Eyes Across a Room

I didn't wanna go to that dance. My heart's been broken enough this year, thank you very much. That's why I spend so much time by myself. George Washington said it's better to be alone than in bad company. And Emerson said nothing can bring you peace but yourself.

I'm fine by myself. Totally fine. But ... intellectually, I recognize that fine is not the same as great. That's why I went to the dance.

And why I stopped in my tracks when I saw two eyes across the room. Two eyes that wouldn't stop looking my way. Like nothing I ever saw before. Nobody ever looked at me like that. Not even the person ... who stomped all over my heart this year.

I walked towards the owner of those eyes. And now I'm so glad I did. Showing up at that dance with a good attitude was our beginning. Don't know how the story ends yet. Can't say where it's going.

But showing up with a good attitude opens up a world of possibilities. And, you know what? I'm showing up with a good attitude more and more these days.

The Beauty of Patience

My mom says we all have to develop more patience. Dad says patience is directly proportional to the number of witnesses and security cameras in the immediate vicinity.

Funny, right? Also true. Most people behave best when they know watchful eyes are upon them. My father included.

Dad's got kind of a hot temper, to tell you the truth. Mom says he used to really have a short fuse. But Dad keeps that temper under control these days. He demonstrates a lot of patience. Apparently, he was a wild man before me and my sisters were born. Dad was a boxer – and a street fighter – in his younger days. But my father says he can't fly off the handle like he did back then. Adult responsibilities now. Wife, kids, house, business. Too much at stake.

And if he loses his temper – he could lose everything. So Dad's right. We do behave best when someone's watching … when there are watchful eyes upon us. Even if those watchful eyes are our very own.

The Beauty of Failure

Don't worry. It's okay. Breathe. You'll be all right. Don't be afraid of failure. It's no biggie. I promise. If the big, bad world knocks you down, you just try something else. Try something new. It's not about making the team. It's not about acing the test. It's not about finding the perfect prom date. It's not about knocking it out of the park. It's about your willingness to try ... even if you may fail. Even if you fall flat on your face.

Because failure tells people something important about you. Failure demonstrates that you were out in the big, bad world attempting to do something significant with your life. Winston Churchill said success is going from failure to failure without losing your enthusiasm.

So put on your big boy pants. Put on your big girl pants. And when life knocks you down, get up and try again. You may not win every time, but you may just learn something amazing. You may just learn you're a whole lot stronger and more resilient than you thought you could be. And that's not such a bad lesson to learn once in a while.

The Power of Focus

You know, it's very easy to get distracted these days. There's just so much stuff going on in this world ... to pull every one of us in a hundred seventy-four different directions.

That's too many directions.

So we gotta pay attention. Focus. Concentrate on one thing. The sun's rays going through a magnifying glass are much more powerful than the sun's rays dispersed all over the place.

Think about the woodpecker. A woodpecker can tap on a thousand different trees and get nowhere. He'll get frustrated, frazzled, and burned-out. Or ... that same woodpecker can tap a thousand times on just one tree and get a nice, tasty dinner for himself. And all his other woodpecker friends too.

But it's the woodpecker's choice. He decides. Focus on one thing or a thousand. You and I can train ourselves up the same way.

Dispersion or attention? Dissipation or laser-like focus? Distraction or dinner?

I choose attention. I choose laser-like focus. I choose dinner.

The Power of Discipline

I have to talk with you about something important. Discipline. That word scares people. In fact, some people think discipline is a dirty word.

It's not.

Because discipline equals correction. Discipline is the process through which we learn and improve. So discipline is not a bad thing. Discipline is actually a very good thing.

Discipline is the tool that helps us improve. Discipline helped Michael Phelps get better at swimming. Discipline helped Steve Jobs create the iPhone. Discipline helped NASA send astronauts to the moon.

Discipline will help you improve in every area of your life. In everything you do. But that's the trick. You have to actually do it.

You have to discipline *yourself*. Self-discipline is the way to go. You can discipline yourself to go out and get stuff done. Don't wait for someone else. You have to provide your own discipline and motivation.

Because the best place in the world to find a helping hand … is at the end of your very own arm. So discipline yourself to look for it right there … where it can help you most.

You're Dangerous

You're dangerous. You're more powerful than you even know. You're the most dangerous person in the world ... to your own happiness and well-being.

Because you're the only one who can de-rail your goals. You're the only one who can talk yourself out of every great dream you have for your life.

And it's up to you whether or not you will.

Why do little kids love athletes so much? I'll tell you why. Because famous athletes never gave up on their dreams. Unlike most of the adults little kids see all around them in this world.

And those athletes don't make excuses. Excuses are like armpits. Everyone has a couple and they all stink.

So when you're feeling down ... when you feel like you've got nothing going on ... just remember how powerful and how dangerous you are.

You're the only person on this planet who can stop your dreams from materializing. And that's one ability, one super-power I hope you never use.

Stop Stopping

I need you to start believing in yourself. I need you to get out of the passenger seat and step boldly forth into the driver seat.

Stop making excuses for why you're not where you want to be. It's not someone else's fault. No. You're not where you want to be because of you! Every time you point a finger, you've got three pointing right back at you.

So stop complaining. Stop griping. Stop whining.

Most of all ... stop stopping. Stop stopping yourself from being the person you know you could be. The person you're truly supposed to be. The person you were always meant to be.

The way our neurology is hard-wired, our brains are designed to protect us from predators, and keep us safe and sound inside our comfort zones. Safety's nice, but it doesn't give you an option to grow, to expand, to step boldly into your destiny. And that's the only way to move forward in life.

We move forward through green lights. Not red lights. So stop stopping yourself. I need – the world needs – all of us to stop stopping.

Dog Tail

I was watching my dog chase his tail ... noticing how easily entertained a sweet, uncomplicated, furry little animal can be. Then I realized I was completely entertaining *myself* watching my dog completely entertaining *himself* ... by chasing his tail.

So I asked myself, "Hey, Self, who's really the sweet, uncomplicated, furry little animal in this equation?" Who's the mammal most easily entertained by this phenomenon of watching another mammal chase its tail? The mammal chasing its tail ... or the one observing ... commenting upon – and performing a monologue about ... the tail chaser?

Please don't answer that question. I think I know. Because there are times when I catch myself ... when I suddenly realize I'm not living up to my own highest standards and expectations.

Like when I find myself doing things that are not smart. Like looking everywhere for my phone ... then realizing it's in my hand. Like turning down the music in the car to help me read the street signs better. Like getting out of that car without unbuckling the seat belt.

So don't laugh at your dog chasing his tail. Maybe somebody's watching ... and laughing at all the goofy things we humans do each day.

Cat Rescue

TNR. Do you know what that stands for? Don't worry. Most people don't. TNR. Trap. Neuter. Release. That's the three-step plan they use in the animal rescue community.

I know because my aunt works in animal rescue. And she's a one-woman army.

She goes out – sometimes at two o'clock, three o'clock in the morning to trap stray cats and get them fixed ... basically so they stop having more stray cats. How does she find out where to go that time of night?

I'm glad you asked that question.

People tell her. People call or email her when they start seeing stray cats in the neighborhood. Wild, huh? The goal – big picture goal – is to reduce the overpopulation of unwanted animals.

And my aunt has become so good at it ... people started calling her from all over Los Angeles, where she lives. That's the second largest city in the U.S., you know? So that's an awesome responsibility. And she's an awesome lady ... doing awesome work in her awesome community.

And ... it's pretty awesome to have her as my aunt too.

Bring Your Own Sardines

My big, bad Uncle Ray is what they call a health nut. Most of the time, anyway.

He watches everything he eats. Wants to make sure he gets enough protein. He says that's important so he can have good workouts in the gym.

But that's not always easy. Sometimes he goes to dinner with his friends and they don't have a healthy menu at the restaurant. That's when Uncle Ray pulls out his super secret weapon.

Sardines.

Right. Sardines. My Uncle Ray carries sardines with him everywhere he goes. You know those little cans with the little fishies squished down inside? Those are sardines. My uncle's favorite. Kinda like tuna fish, only oilier and squishier.

Apparently, sardines are loaded with protein – and all kinds of nutrients for our brains. Sardines. Who would have ever thought those greasy, smelly little fishies would be popular with the workout crowd ... and health nuts like my Uncle Ray?

My big, bad Uncle Ray ... and his little smelly, squishy sardines. What a dream team. What a match made in Healthy Heaven. I think I'll keep him.

Happy To Be Here

My father's got a funny saying. "I'm like the mole on Cindy Crawford's face. Just happy to be here."

Funny, right? Weird, but still funny. It's Dad's way of saying he's happy to be walking around on this planet. Happy to participate. Happy to still be alive. My father had a health issue last year. He's better now … but the doctor said it could have gone either way. Scary.

And Dad takes care of himself. He doesn't smoke. He's not overweight. He plays basketball with the guys from his job. He sure didn't expect to have a health issue. But he sure did.

And that sure changed my father. It taught him a lesson … to be more grateful. Grateful to still be here … with his family … walking around on planet Earth. Given another chance at doing the right thing … living a good life … and making a little bit of a difference in the world … as long as he can.

That's my father. Just happy to still be here … and not be removed … like that mole on Cindy Crawford's face.

My Ex

Ibroke up with someone I really liked. Someone special. Some-one who's now my ex.

Our problem was psychological. My ex is psycho, and I'm logical. Okay, I know I shouldn't make jokes like that. It's not respectful. I guess we're just different. I should have recognized those red flags when they first came up.

My ex loved astrology, horoscopes, stuff like that. Turns out I'm an Earth sign. My ex is a water sign. Together we made mud.

That's not a particularly effective combination. People are supposed to encourage each other … to lift each other up … take each other to new heights. Not drag each other down into all those deep, muddy depths.

Any time we expend too much time, effort, and energy around someone who's not right for us … it shows that we don't value ourselves as we should. We're not placing enough value on our own time, effort, and energy. And that's not the best strategy to attract the right people into our lives.

My uncle says it best. "Go where you're celebrated, not tol-erated."

The Relative Length of a Minute

Got a minute? I want to talk to you for a minute. Can I ask you for a minute of your time?

How long is a minute? I don't know. Depends which side of the bathroom door you're on. Because time is relative. It's different for every person.

A minute spent waiting for a light to turn green might seem like an hour. While a minute spent doing something you love might only feel like a second.

Because it's all relative. It's different for you than it is for me. And it's different for my Uncle Charlie too. And that's okay. Because we're all wildly different. And our differences are what make us interesting as individuals.

Like they say, that's what makes the world go around. But make sure you don't invest time with people and situations that don't value yours. Because some people talk to you in their free time ... and some people free up their time so they can talk to you. Learn to recognize the difference.

Mike Kimmel

Fear is a Liar

What are you afraid of? Is there something making you nervous?

Making your stomach turn in knots? Everyone has something like that. And it's different for each of us.

But fear is a liar. That's right. Whatever is whispering in your ear is not even true. Someone said fear wants you to run from something that's not after you. I think that's exactly right.

It may feel like something's after us in the moment, but that's not true. It's not real. Feelings are not facts. So we shouldn't treat them like facts.

They're imaginary. Like the bogeyman. Like the closet monster. Like the scary thing under the bed when you were little. Remember? When you turned the light on ... you saw there was nothing there.

Fear is like that. It disappears when you shine your light on it. When you expose it for what it really is – nothing.

So when fear rears its ugly head, step forward ... not back. Step up ... not down. Face your fear squarely in the center of the ring.

Look fear right in the eye ... and watch that nasty fear disappear.

It's All in Your Head

Is there something you're a little worried about today? Something bothering you? Something at the back of your mind? Something that's keeping you from moving forward in your life?

I think we all have something like that we're dealing with. Something secret ... and it may be different for every one of us. It's like whatever you were afraid of as a kid. Maybe it was the Chupacabra. Maybe it was the Rougarou. Maybe it was just the plain old everyday monster under your bed. When you turned on the light, you saw that it didn't really exist.

And fear doesn't really exist. Because everything you're afraid of began as a simple thought. Every fear in your life only exists inside the confines of your very own mind.

But fear is an evil trickster ... a manipulator. Fear wants us to run away from something that's not even chasing us. Something that's not even real.

So never trust your fears. They don't know your true strength.

And the next time you feel afraid, the next time you feel fear creeping its way in ... remember your strengths. Remember everything you've overcome in your life up to now.

And make fear ... fear you.

Aunt Stephanie

You should meet my Aunt Stephanie. My very favorite relative. Seriously, you gotta meet her. I'm trying to find her a husband. She's a single mom ... with a twenty-one year old daughter. That happens. We see it a lot nowadays.

Lots of ladies marry the wrong guy. Which is bad enough, but when kids are thrown in ... it complicates things a little bit.

Aunt Stephanie has a unique way of looking at the world. She never calls herself single. Instead, she says, "I'm independently owned and operated." Funny, right? Guess what? She's smart too. Guess what? She's gorgeous too! Doesn't look it, but Aunt Stephanie's forty years old. Says she's not really forty ... she's twenty-year old twins!! Another good one, right?

That's my Aunt Stephanie. Always makes jokes. Always looks on the bright side. Always finds the hidden benefit in a ... less than ideal situation. Yep. That's my Aunt Stephanie. My gorgeous, independently owned and operated, twenty-year old twins ... Aunt Stephanie. My very favorite relative.

And you really should meet her sometime, you know? I'm trying to find her a husband.

Piano Lessons

My parents make me take piano lessons. I guess it's a good discipline …

But it's never been my thing.

Mom and Dad were in the other room watching TV … this concert from way back. From years ago when they were dating. They were laughing so hard … and singing so loud … I couldn't concentrate.

So I went in the living room to watch. It was a piano concert, believe it or not. With two of their favorites … Elton John and Billy Joel totally rocking it out on stage. Hammering away on their pianos like two wild men. So much energy! How do they make that beautiful music come out of … this big, clunky instrument? This same instrument I'm struggling with?

Answer – it's not a big, clunky instrument. It's a beautiful instrument … a harp on its side … I just never saw it … or appreciated it. Until now. Now I have a new found appreciation for the piano. I may never play like Elton John and Billy Joel … but I'll keep practicing until I can play really, really well. I promise I will.

Call Aunt Tammy

There's one in every family. In my family, it's Aunt Tammy. My mom's baby sister. Anytime anyone needs anything – they call Aunt Tammy. My super-smart Aunt Tammy. Mom says she's the smartest one in the whole family. I say she's the smartest one in any family.

Anytime I write a paper, Aunt Tammy proofreads it. Just to catch mistakes – the little grammatical gremlins, as she calls them.

Anytime someone takes a trip, they call Aunt Tammy. She finds them the best deal on the best flight at the best time with all the best options … options the person taking that trip didn't even think of asking for – but always appreciates after Aunt Tammy figures it out for them!

Because Aunt Tammy plans ahead. Aunt Tammy says we have to anticipate every hole in the boat.

And she does it so well, I'm promoting her to Captain. Captain of that boat. And just like a Captain, she's strong, fearless, and in control. She can navigate the family through all kinds of rough waters – and bring every crew member back home safe and sound … with perfect spelling, perfect grammar, and perfect punctuation!

Three Weeks

Wanna hear something crazy? My grandma and grandpa knew each other for three weeks when they got married. Three weeks.

Nowadays ... it takes people three weeks just to figure out if they like each other. To decide if they're gonna have a second date.

Okay. Maybe I'm exaggerating a little ... but not by much.

Seriously ... doesn't it feel like we've lost something? My entire generation, I mean. I don't wanna be rude, but it seems like we just don't get stuff done like people did back in the day. In my grandparents' generation, I mean.

Grandpa worked two jobs and went to school at night. Grandma raised eight small children – and took in sewing and ironing to bring in a little extra cash at home.

How the heck did they do it? Commitment, that's how the heck they did it.

Total one hundred percent commitment to each other, their family, and their future. My grandparents have been married fifty years. And it all started from a three-week courtship. Now that's what I call commitment.

A Good Day for a Good Day

Do you know what today is? I'm not just looking for the standard answer, either. Today is something special. It's a gift. That's why we call it the present. Today is a really good day to have a really good day.

Today is a day ripe with possibilities. If you imagine yourself as a sculptor, today is like clay. You can mold it into any shape you'd like. If you're a painter, today is a canvas you can paint your masterpiece upon. You decide. It's up to you every day. You're the artist.

Carlos Castaneda was a great writer. He said we make ourselves happy or we make ourselves miserable. It's the same amount of work. And it's always up to us.

My favorite book says we should rejoice in this day. We should be glad in this day. Rejoice and be glad? Those are good instructions. Pretty good way to make sure we make ourselves happy and not miserable. Pretty good way to make sure it's a really good day to have a really good day.

Mistakes Are Our Friends

Practice makes ... absolutely not! Practice only makes you better. A lot of people say they don't want to do anything until they can do it perfectly. How many people do you know who can do anything perfectly?

Me neither. Because you have to be willing to make mistakes and keep on making them until you get better. Understand? Better, not perfect.

Making mistakes is the only way to learn ... and it's necessarily a very active process. You can't learn how to swim by watching videos of Michael Phelps swimming. You've got to jump in there and blub around a few times.

That's the learning process. And it's the same for me, you, and everyone else out there who's trying to learn something new or accomplish anything worthwhile in life.

Don't be afraid of making mistakes. Remember – you make mistakes, mistakes don't make you.

Stories Better Left Untold

There's this girl in my school. Really sweet … but also really sad. Always looks like she just stopped crying. You know that look? She's usually by herself. I see her alone a lot. Her clothes never look right. Sometimes she looks dirty … and even smells a little.

Boy, there must be some story there. Maybe some stories are better left untold. Some questions are better left unanswered. Like … how did she get this way?

Sometimes in life, we don't know what to do … so we do nothing. We may not have an answer … but someone does. And we can do a world of good for a person who's struggling … a person who's hurting … when we step out of our comfort zones and that find someone who can help.

Maybe some stories are better left untold, but we can tell them to a teacher, or a counselor … or a school administrator.

I used to look at this girl and think to myself … somebody should do something. Somebody should help that kid. Somebody should make a call.

Then I said to myself … "Hey, I'm somebody."

And you're somebody too.

Trevor the Tall

There's this sixteen-year-old kid who lives down the block from me. Trevor. Super tall and thin. Looks like a long, lean cowboy from one of those old John Wayne movies.

We call him Trevor the Tall.

Because he's ... super tall ... obviously. He's the tallest one in his family. Much taller. He towers over everyone. He doesn't look like the rest of the family either.

There's a good reason. He's adopted. That's why.

Jennifer and Sammy adopted him when he was thirteen years old. They knew his grandfather. They also knew there were family challenges, so they stepped up and welcomed him into their home before the government could come in and take him away.

That's not an easy thing to do. Especially because they have three daughters at home. A lot of married couples would worry about their daughters.

But they don't have anything to worry about with Trevor the Tall. He's turned out to be an awesome addition to the family. And those girls now have an awesome little brother too. Or an awesome ... *big* brother ... because he keeps getting taller and taller every day!

Why Dress Like That?

Iwas watching this girl at the coffee shop. The one we always go to after school. She was about our age, but I don't think she goes to our school. Pretty sure I never saw her before. Pretty sure I'd remember this girl.

Very pretty, but what was really interesting about her … was, uh, her pants. Yeah, her pants. How do I say this nicely? Her pants were so tight, I don't know how she even got them on. They were so tight, I could practically see how much change she had in her pockets.

That's way too tight. That's just not right.

Why wear pants that tight? Why dress that way? Just to show off? Just to say, "Look at me?" I don't get it. This girl was really pretty too, but what she was wearing to show off how pretty she was … was distracting my attention from how pretty she was! I'd rather look at her face. I'd rather look at her smile. She had such a nice smile too.

Kinda defeats its own purpose. If your goal in life is to just look pretty … then just look pretty in something more comfortable. Something not so tight. Maybe something that shows off that smile. Why dress like that?

My Gorgeous Teacher

You ought to see my teacher. All the boys have a huge, gigantic crush on her. And no wonder. She is absolutely gorgeous. Looks like she stepped off the cover of a magazine.

And she dresses real nice. Not too ... provocative ... if you know what I mean. Kinda conservative, actually. She's always completely covered up.

But she's so beautiful ... guys are just naturally gonna look. Some guys in my class say they can't concentrate on their schoolwork. Because she looks the way she does!

But that's not her fault. That's on them. She can't help that she's pretty. Just means she has a pretty mother and a handsome father. Right? Something she can't even control. And how hard is this to figure out, by the way?

Not too difficult. But these kids want to blame our gorgeous teacher because they can't pay attention in school. That's totally unfair. In fact, that's just plain rude too. It must be hard for a woman to be that pretty.

And it makes me wonder ... if men her own age treat her that same way too?

The Multiplication of Geometry

We have to do more in life. All of us. Ghandi said the difference between what we are capable of and what we actually do … could solve most of the world's problems .

When I heard that, it really made me think.

We all have to multiply our efforts. Myself included. I was having trouble in math this session. We're doing geometry.

I started thinking … when am I ever gonna use geometry?! But that's exactly the wrong approach. Definitely the wrong question to ask.

A better question would be … "How can I learn something here … and make the most of this situation … even if I don't see an immediate application?"

So I started hunkering down. Getting real serious with my studies. Looking for extra geometry problems. Asking my teacher for more assignments. Doing extra credit. Eating, drinking, breathing, and sleeping geometry.

What do you think happened? Correct!

Guess who got an A in geometry this session? Correct again! Boy, you're smart. I am happy to report that me and Pythagoras are now best friends. BFFs for sure. We're good to go.

Pluses and Minuses

Is anything perfect in your life?

Nope. Me neither. Seems like there's always some good ... but then again ... there's always some kinda bad.

Pluses and minuses. Like this girl in my math class ... she's probably the prettiest girl in the whole school ... but her family situation at home is terrible. Pluses and Minuses.

And my study partner Jeffrey gets straight A's in all his classes ... but he's very shy. He feels completely clueless in the dating world. Pluses and Minuses.

My grandma says you can have everything in life ... you can have it all ... just not at the same time. She says we all have problems ... but if everyone in the world put their problems out there in the open air ... for everyone else to see and compare with our own ... we'd all choose to keep the ones we already have!!

Because we all have pluses and minuses. Just try your best to keep them in perspective. And try your best to make sure one of your pluses ... is your own good attitude.

Rookie of the Year

My uncle was rookie of the year. Before I was born, he was rookie of the year. In a most unusual sport. Professional wrestling. Yeah, yeah, I know.

Some people love it. Some people hate it. But professional wrestling is one brutally tough game. Definitely not for babies.

My uncle could handle it ... or thought he could. He was on the wrestling team in high school and college. Competed in judo, weightlifting, other sports. But pro wrestling ... is a whole different animal entirely.

Yep. It's an animal, all right. He got injured. All the guys did. Back, neck, shoulders, knees, elbows. I asked ... how did you get all these injuries?

I'll never forget his answer. "I had help." His opponents, he meant. It's scary how they beat each other half to death. All for the roar of the crowd.

Now that crowd's gone. The aches and pains remain. I wonder how many hardcore wrestling fans would recognize my uncle as that young, strong, proud rookie of the year ... raising that great, big trophy overhead ... when they see him now with that great big ice pack on his neck.

Recommended Reading

Acting in Film by Michael Caine
The Actor's Scenebook by Michael Shulman and Eva Mekler
Adventures in the Screen Trade by William Goldman
The Art of Acting by Stella Adler
As a Man Thinketh by James Allen
Audition by Michael Shurtleff
Audition and Book It! by Helen McCready
Being an Actor by Simon Callow
The Courage to Create by Rollo May
How I Made A Hundred Movies in Hollywood
    and Never Lost a Dime by Roger Corman
How to Act & Eat at the Same Time by Tom Logan
How to Audition on Camera by Sharon Bialy
How to Stop Worrying and Start Living by Dale Carnegie
IMPRO: Improvisation and the Theatre
    by Keith Johnstone
Know Small Parts by Laura Cayouette
Letters to a Young Actor by Robert Brustein
Letters to a Young Artist by Anna Deavere Smith
Live Cinema by Francis Ford Coppola
100 Ways to Motivate Yourself by Steve Chandler
Tips: Ideas for Actors by Jon Jory
The Ultimate Scene and Monologue Sourcebook
    by Ed Hooks

About Paris Smith

Aproud member of SAG-AFTRA and the Television Academy (Emmys), twenty-year old Paris Smith has already
acted in dozens of plays, musicals, TV shows, and films. She
is best known for her series regular role as Maddie Van Pelt,
one of the stars of Nickelodeon's popular *Every Witch Way* (84
episodes), for which she won a 2015 Young Artist Award and
a 2016 Young Entertainer Award for Best Leading Actress in
a TV Series. Paris guest-starred in Nickelodeon's *Talia and the
Kitchen, Nicky, Ricky, Dicky, and Dawn,* and in 2018, she returned to
Nickelodeon as Princess Dimples on the series *Knight Squad.* She
recurred in the Fine Brothers' Emmy Award–winning YouTube
series *Kids React,* continuing as her character when the show
became a hit on Nickelodeon as *React To That.* Her network
credits include CBS' *Modern Family*, ABC's *Speechless*, and NBC's
Superstore. She has starred in the Lifetime Network films *A Stolen
Life*, for which she won a 2019 Young Entertainer Award for
Best Leading Young Actress in a Television Movie, as well as *My
Stepfather's Secret.* She also played a supporting role in Lifetime's
Deadly Daughter Switch. Her other recent work includes the West-
ern drama *A Soldier's Revenge,* alongside AnnaLynne McCord,
Neal Bledsoe, and Val Kilmer.

Before she moved to Los Angeles at 11 years old, Paris began
acting at an early age in her hometown of Houston, TX, where
she appeared in TV commercials, performed in stage productions including *The Wizard of Oz* and *The Sound of Music*, both
produced by Theatre Under The Stars, as well as *Hello Dolly*

and *Joseph and the Amazing Technicolor Dreamcoat*. She later landed a role in the feature film *Puncture* alongside Chris Evans and Vinessa Shaw.

Paris writes and performs original music, and has released three singles on iTunes (Crush on Hollywood, He Says, and Game Over) and two additional songs on YouTube (Swagger and Tattoo You). Paris also trains in a variety of dance styles, including contemporary, ballet, jazz, and hip hop – and has performed competitively with the Independence Dance Company.

Paris has a dog named Bella and supports the ASPCA and Kinder4Rescue. She works with other charitable organizations including Say NO Bullying and The Shoe Crew, and grows food in her backyard for her local Food Bank. Paris has also worked with the Ronald McDonald House on a variety of fundraising events.

Paris is currently studying acting at the University of Southern California, and was inducted into the Alpha Lambda Delta National Honor Society. She also studies at the Lee Strasberg Theatre & Film Institute in New York City. Paris auditioned for and was accepted into the Royal Academy of Dramatic Art (RADA) in London and looks forward to attending their intensive 8-week Shakespeare course.

About Mike Kimmel

Mike Kimmel is a film, television, stage, and commercial actor and acting coach. He is a twenty-plus year member of SAG-AFTRA with extensive experience in both the New York and Los Angeles markets. He has worked with directors Francis Ford Coppola, Robert Townsend, Craig Shapiro, and Christopher Cain among many others. TV credits include *Game of Silence*, *Zoo*, *Treme*, *In Plain Sight*, *Cold Case*, *Breakout Kings*, *Memphis Beat*, *Buffy The Vampire Slayer*, and *The Oprah Winfrey Show*. He was a regular sketch comedy player on *The Tonight Show*, performing live on stage and in pre-taped segments with Jay Leno for eleven years.

Mike has appeared in dozens of theatrical plays on both coasts, including Radio City Music Hall, Equity Library Theater, Stella Adler Theater, Double Image Theater, The Village Gate, and Theater at the Improv. He trained with Michael Shurtleff, William Hickey, Ralph Marrero, Gloria Maddox, Harold Sylvester, Wendy Davis, Amy Hunter, Bob Collier, and Stuart Robinson. He holds a B.A. from Brandeis University and an M.A. from California State University at Dominguez Hills.

He has taught at Upper Iowa University, University of New Orleans, University of Phoenix, Glendale Community College, Nunez Community College, Delgado Community College, and in the Los Angeles, Beverly Hills, and Burbank, California public school districts. He is a two-time past president of New Orleans Toastmasters, the public speaking organization, and often serves as an international speech contest judge. Mike has written and collaborated on numerous scripts for stage and screen. *In Lincoln's Footsteps*, his full-length historical drama on Presidents Lincoln and Garfield, was a semi-finalist in the National Playwrights Conference at the Eugene O'Neill Theater Center. Mike also received the Excellence in Teaching Award from Upper Iowa University in 2014.

Mike is a full voting member of the National Academy of Television Arts and Sciences, the organization that produces the Emmy Awards. He is the author of *Scenes for Teens*, *Acting Scenes for Kids and Tweens*, *Monologues for Teens*, *Monologues for Kids and Tweens*, and *Six Critical Essays on Film*.

In 2019, the Independent Author Network selected *Monologues for Teens*, Mike's third published book, as their Performing Arts Book of the Year. Mike is also featured in Francis Ford Coppola's groundbreaking 2017 book, *Live Cinema*.

"Do not let the hero in your soul perish, in lonely frustration, for the life you deserved but never have been able to reach. Check your road and the nature of your battle. The world you desired can be won. It exists, it is real, it is possible, it is yours."

~ Ayn Rand

Made in the USA
Monee, IL
04 December 2022

19589495R00079